HOME
FOR HOSTS
STAY
101

The Complete Guide
to Start and Run
a Successful Homestay!

By Cheryl Verstrate

Dedicated to
Mark, Sean and Paige

Contents

Homestay 101: Introduction

Today's NEW Landlord

Have you ever wondered what it would be like to welcome world travelers to share your Home-Sweet-Home? Can you picture yourself using your hosting, cooking and decorating ideas to bring unforgettable memories to an International Guest? As a **Homestay Host,** you can live in and work from your home, as well as meet new and interesting visitors from all over the world!

> "Culture-Travel" has created its own industry!

An empty bedroom or two or maybe even three! A guesthouse or maybe an entire apartment! All of these vacant rooms can become Guest accommodations and work to earn some additional income. Guests will stay and are prepared to pay for the comfort of your home.

In our busy, often chaotic world of juggling work and family, many people are re-examining their ideals, priorities and lifestyles. With inflation, taxes and the cost of owning and running a home increasing, more and more people are looking for alternative ways to supplement their income by working from their home. For many homeowners Homestay is the answer!

"Culture-Travel" has created its own industry! With international boundaries lifting, the nations of the world are blending together, creating this wonderful cultural fusion. Countless young people are continuing their post-secondary education abroad. Many interns, working professionals and exploring adults are traveling by using work, student and visitor visas to increase their experience with other cultures and languages. A great many of these International Guests are coming to Canada, the U.S., Europe, Australia and New Zealand.

Although we don't think of education as an industry, that's exactly what it is. And, on a worldwide scale, it is worth billions! With all this currency arriving into the local economies, homeowners are opening

up their doors and welcoming this cultural exchange and opportunities provided by these foreign visitors.

Homestay provides the opportunity to use that extra bedroom as Guest accommodation and offer a safe, welcoming home-away-from–home environment for International Visitors from around the world. What a great way to really get to know people from other cultures *and* to put your home to work!

There is such an increased demand for Homestay accommodation it has become the fastest growing segment of the accommodation industry. It is the most often-used manner of accommodation for overseas Guests. Countless people are inviting these Guests to stay in their homes.

> Homestay is the most often frequently used manner of accommodation for overseas Guests.

With Homestay accommodation being so popular in most industrialized countries, it is surprising that there is so little information available. Whether you explore the library or the Internet, the information specific to hosting a Homestay Guest has been very limited. The best advice typically comes from other Homestay Hosts themselves.

With information on setting up and running a Homestay so scarce, many potential or new Homestay Hosts find they have little resources to guide them through the process. That is where this guide comes in.

Between the pages of this book are useful and valuable tips, pros and cons, as well as words of wisdom gathered from numerous experienced Homestay Hosts. After reading this book, you will be able to make an educated decision about running a Homestay Home and will be equipped with the information you need to establish a successful start to your Homestay. Even if you have already experienced the magic of hosting an International Guest, you will find this book to be a powerful resource.

The QUIET GIANT

Gone are the days when exchange students were just that – exchanging students for a two-week period from one country to another. These days, International students are a billion dollar industry. According to various industry sources:

- One student can spend a total of $30,000 annually on tuition, living expenses, meals and recreation. This means that 1,000 students can spend $30-million annually. This is a significant influx of dollars into a community. The economic spin-offs of international education are huge!

- Although we don't often think of education as an industry, that's exactly what it is! It is **serious** big business that can be worth billions to the economy.

- International schools are a big market. Many new or existing schools are joining in to capitalize on this booming industry.

- Close to 700 million people worldwide travel each year, and that number is expected to double to 1.4 billion people by the year 2020.

That's why we like to call the Homestay industry **THE QUIET GIANT** … these numbers are staggering!

Personally Speaking

For more than 15 years, my family and I have been successfully hosting students, interns and visiting professionals in our home. Over the years we have enriched our lives with the special experience of each of our International Guests and, in doing so we have developed this incredible Global Family.

Our knowledge is a family affair! We have received many of our International Guests through recommendations of previous Guests and through local international schools. With a family history in the hotel and accommodation business, we bring great ideas and tips to help you start-up and run a successful Homestay.

While working as a Homestay coordinator for an international school, I have put together suitable matches for Homestays Hosts and Guests and, when needed, act as a liaison between the Host and Guest to help work through any situations that would arise. I have been a cultural adviser for both hosts and students over the years, and continue to do so today.

> A simple calculation:
> Trial + Error =
> Experience and Knowledge

Books on the topic of running a Homestay business are almost non-existent. Many people who want to become Homestay Hosts can find little or no information. The schools and agencies provide only basic guidelines for the Hosts. Most of the websites available are designed to provide information to students and international visitors and provide only small amounts of information geared to the Host. Therefore, Homestay Hosts had to rely on trial-and-error, with nothing to guide them through the process.

> As experienced Homestay hosts, we receive many phone calls asking our advice. Throughout the years we have shared our knowledge and experiences, we came to realize how little information is available.

Out of frustration and necessity, this informative guide has come about. With my years of experience as a Homestay Host and many real-life situations, both Hosts and Guests urged me to write this helpful guide.

This book is designed to share my own expertise, as well as that of other hosts, in an easy-to-understand, everyday language. It is intended to be a useful reference in answering the HOW TO and everyday questions for all Homestay Hosts!

How This Guide Will Help You

Culture Travel has become extremely popular with International students and traveling visitors who look forward to living and experiencing another culture. Homestay is their preferred means of accommodation. With this increasing appeal for Homestay, numerous homeowners have entered this new home-based business by opening up their homes with no advice to guide them through the process!

That's where this book comes in.

There are many reasons for wanting to become a Homestay Host: to escape the corporate treadmill; to be a stay-at-home mom; to achieve early retirement; the off-season for your B&B, or perhaps you just want to meet new people from around the world! While many people host for personal fulfillment, others host in order to achieve financial gain.

Today, more and more people are looking for ways to supplement their income. Running a home-based business as a Homestay Host can offer flexibility and freedom from the so-called 9 to 5 J-O-B. You also have the option of hosting part-time or year-round.

You ask, "What does it take to be a Homestay Host?" and "How do I get started?" In this book, I will show you how to start, organize and set up your home for running a Homestay.

How do I start?
What is involved?
HOW DO I DO THIS?

We interviewed dozens of Hosts for real-life situations and answered many questions? We have also added useful work sheets and check lists to get you going and organized. This book is a valuable tool to help guide and prepare you through the Homestay Host process.

Running your home as a Homestay is not for everyone, and it is not always easy! If you are already a Homestay Host, operate a seasonal bed and breakfast, or just want to find what Homestay is all about, then I know you will find this book full of helpful information, tips and advice. After you read this book, you will have an understanding of the ins and outs of what it takes to be a Homestay Host.

Homestay can be rewarding and a great way to earn extra money, as well as a window to the world and a wonderful way to broaden your horizons from different cultures first hand!

I hope you will read this book to get you started and pick it up when you need some support.

For more information and useful links, see:

www.homestaycentral.com

Defining Homestay

What exactly is Homestay?

The first thing we need to do is explain what exactly a Homestay Home is!

> Homestay is a home-away-from-home.

Homestay is not a hotel, a motel, nor a typical B&B. Homestay is a non-commercialized, private residence with paying Guest(s) who enjoy staying in the comfort and security of a family home. Further, these guests will reside in the family home for an extended period of time, months or sometimes even years.

Homestay takes place in a homeowner–occupied private residence, where the primary purpose of the home is the residence, and the secondary purpose is providing accommodation to a few paying guests. It is safe, affordable housing for international students, interns, traveling professionals and adult visitors from other countries, who are looking to experience and learn your lifestyle. Homestay is a home-away-from-home.

A Homestay is typically located in a residential area, where the Homestay Host welcomes one or more Guests to share their home. The homeowner may have one or more rooms to rent. It is usually a very relaxed type of accommodation, keeping the majority of space for the Host family. Homestay is comparable to the bed and breakfast that is so popular in European countries.

Many people believe that it is illegal to rent out part of their residence. In most jurisdictions, it is perfectly legal to share your house with a limited number of unrelated people who pay rent. Your local zoning office can help you out and can answer any questions you may have.

Homestay is designed to promote a cross-culture living experience, language development and promote new international friendships between local families and visitors from other countries. Foreigners do not need to stay in hotels, apartments or dormitories and spend huge amounts of money. Instead, they can stay in a Host home at a much lower cost, as well as learn and live the culture up close!

> Homestay is designed to promote a cross-culture living experience

The interest and/or objectives of each Guest will vary, and their stay will range from a few days, to weeks, months or even several years. Some long-term International Guests may wish to reside in your home for the full duration of their stay.

Most Host homes are registered with one or more post-secondary, university-type schools that inspect them, but rarely are they required to undergo licensing or inspection by local government agencies (Check with your local municipality). Some Hosts advertise in local newspapers or on websites such as www.homestaycentral.com

The key requirement for your International Guests is a clean room or rooms, with a comfortable bed and study area with the property surroundings tidy and attractive. A private or shared Guest bathroom is also essential.

> The Homestay Host is generally interested in meeting new people.

The Homestay Host is generally interested in meeting new people, experiencing another person's culture and making some additional income while continuing their present employment or retirement.

A Homestay can be in the suburbs, the city, the country or even on a small island. Running a Homestay is a great way to meet new and interesting people from all over the world. What is truly great is that all Homestay Hosts can live and earn that extra income at the place they love the most: Home.

Who Are Homestay Hosts?

Homestay Hosts come from all walks of life.

Homestay Hosts do not have to be a traditional nuclear family. Every Host family is different, just as every Host situation is different.

Singles, couples, one- or two-parent families with children, couples with no children, families with young children or teenage children, extended families with live-in relatives, people with or without pets , many different races, nationalities and religions, the employed, retirees, Baby Boomers looking to supplement their income, and empty nesters find this to be the perfect solution to utilize that empty space.

> Homestay Hosts have the space and feel that they and their family will benefit ... Every Host family is unique.

Homestay Hosts have that extra space and feel that their family will benefit from this cross culture exchange experience. Every Host family is unique. Some are casual and some more formal; some Hosts offer a more relaxed home style while others are a little more rigid. There is one thing that Host families have in common is that they love to meet new and interesting people and welcome them into their homes.

Often, parents of young children find hosting an ideal way to bring in extra income while staying home with the family. Retirees find being a Host is a way to utilize an empty house after their children are grown and gone, and that the company is a bonus. Singles offer to share their accommodations to help out with their living expenses. Writers and artists find the freedom to work on their craft while a consultant runs their new home office, and farmers welcome a second source of income.

> I loved the fact that we were able to go to all the kid's school activities. I didn't end my day being so tired from outside work that our family time was limited.

Personally, I love having the freedom to pursue other interests.

Who Are the Homestay Guests?

Students, interns and visiting professionals are just a few of the International Guests that prefer Homestay as their means of accommodation. There is a good chance that someone you know has hosted a student or traveling visitor from another country. Maybe it was a neighbor, friend or colleague, or perhaps you have hosted one of these young ambassadors yourself. Homestay is one of the big selling points in the language industry, with Home being the most important word.

Not all Homestay Guests are students, but students are a very big part of this ever-growing group of cultural visitors. Other types of Guests include women's alumni groups, various professional groups, tourist groups looking to live and explore locally, or even people who want to work in a foreign country during their travels. These are examples of part of this growing trend where potential Guests wish to live the experience of a different lifestyle in the comforts of a family home.

> Homestay Guests range from 15 years to 75 years. They come with great curiosity, anticipation and enthusiasm ...

Overseas Guests feel they have more exposure to the language and to the culture in a Homestay environment. They would not get the same exposure if they were to move into an apartment or by living in a campus residence. This is their chance to develop the language and learn the way of life at a faster pace from this cross-cultural experience. Living in a Homestay environment familiarizes the Guest with the local area and helps to improve their language skills by correcting grammar and pronunciation.

Homestay Guests range from all ages, 15 years to 75 years. They come with great curiosity, anticipation and enthusiasm and want to consume every inch of our culture and life style.

Hosts can register their accommodations for Guests at www.homestaycentral.com

International Students

International students are a major part of this global trend. They may apply for an academic program for a school semester or a school year. On acceptance, they will attend an elementary, middle or secondary school (private or public) or a post-secondary college or university.

Some students are minors and vary in age from ages 9 to 17, and are hosted by a legal guardian while living away from home. Younger students can only be hosted in a Homestay Home that offers a complete Homestay style and parental supervision.

Older students who live in Homestay while attending college or university require a Homestay with an approach that is consistent with their age and maturity. International students are studying abroad by the thousands. Each year most arrive with Homestay in mind to help them through the cultural barrier. These students need to interact with people and wish to learn our language and experience our culture. Eighty percent or more of all students and interns use Homestay accommodation to help guide them through the transition of living in a new country. Even if the students are planning to stay in an apartment, they are encouraged to stay in a Homestay for the first several months.

> These young ambassadors
> are some of
> their countries
> hottest, future exports.

Many schools in Canada, the United States and Australia are finding that over half of the student body can be made up of international students. This is a global trend. The many ESL programs in colleges, universities and private-sector schools focus on accommodating these International Guests in our communities.

The international students who wish to attend language schools, business school, colleges and universities are all potential Homestay Guests. As well, international sports camps like to use Homestay for their young athletes in order for them to have a full cultural experience.

Homestay is considered the world's greatest classroom!

What Homestay Is NOT!

A Homestay is not the same as a typical bed and breakfast, where a Guest stays for one or two nights and where a full buffet style breakfast is included in their stay. Homestay is also not a hotel, a motel, nor any other commercialized residence.

Homestay Guests are just that: GUESTS! These Guests are not babysitters or domestic help. As Guests, they should never be expected to mind your children or clean up areas of the home that are not used by them. They are paying Guests. However, some organizations require that Guests help the Hosts with dishes and small household chores. Discuss this with the Homestay organizer on this issue in order to reach a balance.

A Host family should not accept this opportunity for their own advantage. Expecting to provide a companion for children should not be your primary reason for becoming a Homestay Host.

> Homestay Hosts should approach homestay opportunities for the right reasons.

Homestay Guests should not be used as a means to save a difficult marriage or for any financial problems that you may have. Be certain that meeting that next month's mortgage payment or those unpaid bills are not your primary reason for Hosting. I have personally observed situations where there have not been enough funds left at the end of the month to properly care for the Guests. Do not depend on Homestay as your only source of income, at least until you have yourself well established. Remember, your reputation as a good Homestay is at risk and it may be only a matter of time before you are not considered suitable for Homestay.

While most companies try to screen the Homestay Host and the accommodations, this process is not always satisfactory and some unsuitable Hosts do slip through.

The selection of Host families as well as the assignment of the International Guest to a Host home must be done without discrimination. If you have any prejudice against religion, race, sex or color, the Homestay business is not for you.

If you have strong religious beliefs, do not assume that your foreign Guests will conform to your way of thinking or convert to your faith. The Host family must respect their Guest's religious beliefs, or lack thereof.

Homestay Hosts should approach this opportunity for all the right reasons. The most important purpose for a Host family is to be able to share their home and themselves.

It's a Family Affair! Consider Your Family

Homestay is an entire family affair. This new venture can be wonderful for everyone, and even the children can contribute to running the Homestay. However, they must be kept informed! The first thing you need to do before you decide to bring a Guest into your home, it is to consult with everyone residing in the home to discuss the idea of having live-in Guests.

> The most important objective of a Host family is being able to share.

You need to discuss any changes that might take place such as sharing the home and the majority of its contents. All members of the household should be in agreement and you must realize that it must not be just one person's decision.

The most important objective of a Host family is being able to share.

For example, a negative teenager or a spouse who has unenthusiastically agreed could make a very unhappy experience for both Guest and family members. For some family members, a new addition to your home may make them feel disconnected — so talk about it!

In any case, this should be a mutual family decision; all members of the household must be in complete agreement and welcome this new lifestyle change.

Remember: If you are stressed trying to keep everyone happy (family, Guests, etc.) they will all feel it, and no one will be comfortable. This is not a good environment for the Host family or their Guests.

One disadvantage to hosting Guests in your home is that it can mean less family privacy. Also, some Guests require more of your time than others, so you need to organize your time well. Make sure to include special time

with your own family too! Family support and understanding is very crucial when running a busy Homestay home.

I cannot emphasize enough the importance of making sure this is something that you have all agreed upon, so it is enjoyable for everyone involved. Analyze your lifestyle and make an informed decision.

Our Growing Son

Lynn and Rob along with their two children had been hosting international students for the past seven years. Over the years, their son, Mathew had found hosting students to be fun and interesting and enjoyed every new Guest that arrived in their home.

But now at the age of 16, Mathew seemed to not share the same enthusiasm as he did when he was younger. He found his lack of privacy was interfering with his personal life. Sharing the bathroom with other teenagers (who all required so much more bathroom time) became a big issue.

Mathew also found that not being able to do certain things without taking their new Guest with him was another hindrance. He started to complain about wanting more independence. Communication between the students of similar ages was difficult and Mathew no longer wanted to put the time and effort needed into communicating and befriending their Guest.

This busy mom, dealing with the everyday needs of her Guests and home, found that Mathew was becoming more and more resentful. He did not always show respect for their housemate and started to act out, making it difficult for Lynn to keep a happy balance in the home.

The family opted to resign from the hosting program for a while or until they felt that Mathews attitude would improve.

Consideration should always go to the children. They need to feel that this is still their home — a place to have fun with their friends and to just spend some quality time with their family.

Host families can read and share their Homestay experiences in our discussion board/blog at www.homestaycentral.com

Is Homestay for You?

The best way to prepare yourself and family for this new adventure is to start with yourself. Consider what it would be like using all your homey expertise to accommodate guests in your home. People who love to cook and bake, and just spend more time at home, find Homestay to be a great way to use their savoir-faire and put their skills to work.

Being a Homestay Host allows you to focus more energy on your home and family as well as giving you the opportunity to meet people from all over the globe. If you are not a world traveler, it will certainly give you a whole different perspective of how small the world truly is!

Homestay allows you to keep the use of the whole house. Homestay can also be one of the most valued experiences in learning a foreign culture from the perspective of both Guest and Host.

Before you open up your home to Guests, it is vital to be as well informed as possible. Approaching the opportunity with a big heart, curious mind and a great sense of humor goes a long way to creating a successful Homestay.

Take a Test Drive!

Consider trying a short-term Guest for three weeks or less before you decide to do hosting full-time. We strongly recommend that you Host several different, short-term Guests to start with, since the investment is minimal and can save a lot of frustration for everyone involved.

Although every Homestay experience is unique, hosting short-term stays in the beginning will give you and your family a hands-on idea of what it takes. This way, the whole family can contribute to the development of a successful Homestay. Experience has been my best teacher!

Before we begin, you need to answer the questions in the next section to find out if **Homestay is for you!**

So let's get started!

Go Ahead! Test Yourself!

The best way to decide if operating a Homestay is right for you is to evaluate your lifestyle. We have put together a 10-question, self-assessment quiz to help measure your potential in becoming a Homestay Host so that you can decide if it is for you. Go ahead and find out if you have what it takes.

Are you social and enjoy meeting new people?	❑ Yes	❑ No
Do you have one or two Guest bedrooms?	❑ Yes	❑ No
Do you cook and enjoy it?	❑ Yes	❑ No
Are you a well-organized person?	❑ Yes	❑ No
Do you tend to stay calm and not over-react to unexpected situations that may arise?	❑ Yes	❑ No
ROOMS? Would YOU honestly be comfortable enough to stay in the Guest room you have to offer for a long period of time?	❑ Yes	❑ No
Can you offer a safe, healthy environment for all Guests?	❑ Yes	❑ No
Does everyone in the house welcome the idea of sharing their home with Guests?	❑ Yes	❑ No
Are you willing and able to be open-minded in the company of cultural differences? Are you willing to try new things and accept new ideas?	❑ Yes	❑ No
Do you and your family have the time to communicate and include your Guest in your family environment?	❑ Yes	❑ No

Hosting International Guests can be rewarding and challenging at times. If you can answer yes to all of the above questions, Homestay Hosting may be ideal for you!

Homestay 101

Do Your Homework!

Preparation is important! The first thing I tell all new Homestay Hosts is: "Do your homework!" Don't presume you already know what to expect just by running a household for years!

As with any type of accommodation business, there are unique situations that you need to be prepared for. It is important to note that every municipality or community has different regulations. It is worthwhile to find out what is regulated for your area. As well, proper insurance policies should be in place before offering any accommodation service.

This step-by-step checklist will help guide you through the process.

- ❑ Evaluate your lifestyle!
- ❑ Total family agreement
- ❑ Check with your municipality/zoning
- ❑ Check your insurance policies
- ❑ Choose your Homestay style
- ❑ Prepare your Homestay space
- ❑ Prepare your home
- ❑ Organize your Homestay business
- ❑ Market your Homestay
- ❑ Contact the Homestay organizations/schools
- ❑ Prepare to welcome your Guests
- ❑ Complete the Cycle

Choosing your Homestay style

Homestay offers different options to suit most lifestyles. There are long-stay Guests and short-stay Guests, older Guests and younger Guests.

There are *All Inclusive Full Homestays* or a *No Frills* basic type of Homestay. There are many ways to fit homestay into **your lifestyle.**

You can offer *Self-catering,* where guests have access to a kitchen to prepare their own meals. There is also *Half-board,* which includes breakfast and/or dinner. Of course, there is the ever-popular *Full Homestay,* where the Guest will share three meals a day with you and your family.

How much or how little interaction you have with your Guests will depend on the style of your Homestay.

> I found that having a Homestay Home allowed me to be home more often and watch my kids grow up. I was able to spend more time with family and friends and found the time to write my book. It would not have been possible without welcoming International Guests into my home.

The Homestay program is designed to provide an opportunity for cultural exchange between local families and visitors from other countries. Their objectives can range across a whole spectrum of interests, as can their length of stay. Some Guests may stay for only a few weeks or months, to more than a few years. Find the comfort zone for you and your family when you decide how to set things up.

To B or not to B … whether setting your Homestay up as a boarding house or as a Bed & Breakfast, Homestay can be professionally run and still be that home away from home! Review the following types of Homestays to help you decide on your Homestay style.

What's the difference between Short-stay & Long-stay?

A *Short-stay* is a one- to four-week program designed for students, youth groups and traveling tourists. Short-stay programs are most often offered in the summer, but can also take place during the winter months. It is customized to incorporate cultural exchange and recreational activities, sightseeing and Homestay accommodation.

> Guests can vary
> from 9 to 75
> years of age.

Some Guests are here to attend an ESL program and experience the culture. Others may be here on an adventure holiday, living the lifestyle and exploring our world. These Guests can vary from 9 to 75 years of age. For the Short-stay programs, you may be required to drop off and pick up your Guest daily.

The shorter program is a great way to begin your Homestay experience. It gives you the opportunity to welcome Guests into your home and get a feel for what it is like to house an overseas Guest.

Long-stay students and working professionals apply for a visa that allows them to stay for one or more years.

All Inclusive Full-Home Homestay

This is the most common type of Homestay and is an owner-occupied private residence. Many Guests choose this style of accommodation for the home comforts, family atmosphere and a chance to practice their English. This is very popular with students studying abroad.

The Typical Full-Home Homestay offers:

- Private bedroom
- Desk or study area with Internet connection
- Private, semi-private or shared bathroom
- Fruit, noodles etc. available for snacks
- Three meals a day including breakfast, lunch (usually a bagged lunch) and a full dinner shared with the family
- Full access to the main parts of the house, including TV family room, kitchen, laundry, etc.
- A total immersion with the family (as living with the family is the greatest way to learn the culture)

Professional Homestay

This style of homestay is a more demanding then most types of Homestay. *Professional Homestay* Hosts must be qualified to offer this type of accommodation. The cost to the Guest is substantially higher than a typical homestay accommodation.

These Guests are often students who are accountable to their parents or educational sponsors while living in a Professional Homestay. The Hosts will submit a monthly report to the parents or sponsors in order to provide an accurate update on the students' educational performance, oversee their financial management, and personal adjustments to their new environment.

A Professional Homestay offers:

- Private bedroom
- Desk or study area with Internet connection
- Private, semi-private or shared bathroom
- Fruit, noodles etc. available for snacks
- Three meals a day including breakfast, lunch (usually a bagged lunch) and a full dinner shared with the family
- Full access to the main parts of the house, including TV family room, kitchen, laundry, etc.
- **Financial Supervision** including financial advice, budgeting, banking, money allocation and disbursements which will be administered as negotiated with parents or sponsors
- **Educational Support** where the Homestay Hosts closely monitors and supports the students in their educational studies in order to ensure the students successfully complete their educational objectives
- Other services such as transportation and most recreational arrangements
- A total immersion with the family

Please remember that it is the **full-time job of the Professional Homestay Host** to guide, care for and ensure that the student completes his or her education and makes the most of their overseas experience.

Room Only or Half-board Homestay

There are Guests that welcome the security that Homestay offers, but are on a tighter budget. A *Room Only* or *Half-board* Homestay is an economical stay that works for them, as there are no extras involved. The Guest expects little interaction with Host family.

An Economy Homestay usually offers:

- Shared or private bedroom
- Shared bathroom (usually with household members/other guests)
- Desk or study area
- Optional meals and food
- Cooking facilities
- Proper food storage facilities

The Homestay Host can decide with the Guest what option to take, such as: (1) no meals, (2) one meal per day or (3) cooking facilities, where they supply their own food and have access to kitchen facilities. Self-catering is very popular with working professionals and some frugal students.

Of course, this is something you have to discuss at the beginning so you can work out a fee that works for both the Host and Guest.

To B or not to B

A *Bed & Breakfast* Homestay/Luxury Homestay (B&B) is an owner-occupied home with a few paying Guests. This has a higher fee for this style of catered-to accommodation. This type of accommodation is generally found in an exclusive neighborhood with close access to all shopping amenities, transportation and local tourist attractions.

This Homestay offers:

- A deluxe private room or suite
- Desk or study area with Internet connection.
- Private or shared bathroom.
- A private entrance (in some cases)
- A self-serve breakfast continental style - cold cereals, breads, milk, juice yogurt and/or fruit. Lunch or dinner is **not usually** provided.

- Access to a washing machine and dryer.
- Access to a private storage area for food and a small fridge.
- Daily clean linen/ blankets and toiletries.

This can be a self-contained suite and more than one Guest could occupy this space. The price of accommodation is reflected in the type of services supplied.

Boarding House Homestay

Also known as a *Study House* or *Quiet House*, this type of home usually accommodates three or more students and/or working guests (I have seen homes where there are up to eight Guests rooms). Of course, this style is run differently than the others.

- Suitable for the more serious student where there are no frills and a less expensive accommodation is required
- Not always a family home - in most cases this is a second home with little supervision
- Since this accommodation usually does not have a homeowner living in the home, it is advisable for it to be well monitored with curfews and a no-guest policy, etc.
- There should be well-defined house rules
- Guests are independent and are always older students focused totally on their study, or a Guest with a working visa
- A daily home monitor and cleaning person for the common area only

A Boarding House/Homestay should have:

- A bathroom for every two to three students
- More than one kitchen in the home (with accurate separate food storage to service Guests cooking for themselves)
- Self-contained locked rooms (with opening windows)
- Some type of laundry service - can be coined operated washer and dryer or a laundry service offered by Host for an extra fee
- Working smoke detectors throughout the home
- Emergency numbers posted in common area

Farm-stay

A *Farm-stay* is where the Guest is staying out in the country and living the lifestyle that farming brings. It is similar to a typical Homestay where the Guest lives and interacts with family, and offers:

- Private bedroom
- Desk or study area with Internet connection
- Private or semi-private bathroom
- Three meals a day including breakfast, lunch (usually a bagged lunch) and a full dinner shared with the family
- Helping with daily chores (depending on program offered)

The Guest may be going to school (via school bus) or the Homestay Host will be a certified teacher with a home study program in place.

Island-stay

This accommodation is situated on a community island where the Guest has the opportunities to experience this unique life style. It is similar to a typical Homestay or B&B style.

ESL Homestay

ESL Homestay is becoming more popular all the time. This type of Homestay is usually a Host home that is owned and operated by a Host who holds a teaching degree, where they offer English instruction classes in the home for 30 minutes daily, or two to three times a week. The language classes may have an extra fee to the Guest.

A lot of Guests welcome this service as it helps their language skills advance more rapidly. This also helps them prepare for TOFEL exams, which gauge English capabilities. Guests usually attend class or work outside the home during the day.

Mom-Stay

A recent trend in Homestay is for the mother to accompany a younger student for the duration of their stay while the child is studying abroad. A separate, furnished suite or furnished apartment is required in order to provide this type of accommodation for both the parent and child.

Billeting or Bed-Sit

Billeting or *Bed-Sit* are terms more commonly used in Europe, but typically refer to a room for rent.

Other Types of Homestay

There are numerous other ways to operate a Homestay. There is a college in Toronto, Canada that has seen such a boom in foreign students that the college purchased a commercial hotel to house the students, due to lack of accommodations.

... a local college purchased a commercial hotel to house the students, due to lack of accommodations.

Another type of boarding home that has become popular is where the agencies or school will rent or purchase a large home. They fill the rooms up with students from the school and hire a guardian to live in the home with them. The guardian cooks and cleans and does the laundry. The student's only responsibility is to go to school and study, sometimes for up to 10 hours a day.

Preparing the Space

A Great Guest Room

The room you are renting to your Guests is one of the most important parts of running a Homestay. Your Guest will spend a great deal of time in their room.

All rooms should be bright and clean, with a working window to the exterior wall. The room should be large enough to accommodate a bed and dresser, a closet and a desk, with some room left over for living space.

> When it comes to renting your room, consider whether or not you would stay in it.
>
> If the answer is NO, the room is NOT rental space.

There are many ways to make the guest room attractive, such as coordinating the room colors with linens, towels, etc. Make an effort to create an inviting, attractive atmosphere. Consider the kinds of things you would like to find in a guest room.

Remember, a fair amount of time is spent in the rooms, so a reasonable amount of moving around space is essential. The room size should be at least 8 feet (2.5 meters) by 10 feet (3 meters) or larger. Proper heat and ventilation are necessary.

Also, all bedrooms must legally have an **OPENING WINDOW** that locks. Each municipality has bylaws dealing with the minimum size and location of opening windows in bedrooms. This is important for fire egress (fire exit).

It is a *private room* — this is the Guest's space and must be respected. Families are requested to respect their Guest's privacy and possessions, so let your Guests know well in advance before entering their room for such things as vacuuming, changing linen or making repairs.

Clean it UP!

Rule # 1 — Keep it clean! Hosts cannot expect a Guest to stay comfortably in their home when it is neglected and uncared for. Having a clean and tidy house adds value to your Homestay and is what your Guest expects. Some people may have a relaxed attitude and do not mind the very lived-in look, but their Guests will not stay long — and why should they? They are paying for a clean, habitable accommodation.

I cannot stress this enough: Do not expect to keep a paying Guest if the house is not kept in a clean and tidy state. Take the time to fix broken furniture and accessories. Housing Guests in your home requires a pride of ownership. Remember, your Guest will tell others of this GREAT Homestay. Being a Host, your emphasis should be on quality and ensure that your Guests are comfortable and happy.

Closets Are For Clothes

Do not assume that you can put a Guest in a room that is no bigger than a closet! **Closets are for clothes**! Be realistic! If it is not usable living space, it should not even be considered. If the space is not a standard size bedroom, it cannot be used as a Homestay room. This is considered storage space and should only be used as such.

> There was an episode in a popular comedy show *(Seinfeld)*, where one of the characters is trying to make some extra cash and has wedged two or three foreign students in big pull out drawers in his very small apartment.
>
> (Of course this is not reality, but you get the idea!)

Common sense tells us that placing a Guest in a drawer or closet is not realistic! Neither is placing a Guest in the farthest, darkest corner of a drafty basement away from the common area of your home. This is not considered suitable for housing a Guest. Imagine coming to a distant country, far from home and your customs, to be placed in a dark, dismal basement room or a closet-size room. This should be a great adventure for the Guest, not a nightmare journey.

No Privacy!

I recall a situation where a young male student had come into the office at the school where I was working, complaining that he was not adjusting well in his new Homestay.

He seemed very distressed, but because the student's English was quite limited, we could not grasp what exactly the problem was. The boy seemed very anxious to leave the Homestay immediately, so we decided to visit his Homestay to try to resolve the problem.

We came to find that the student had been living in a room with no bedroom door. The open space was facing the family room and his bedroom was used as a means of access to a downstairs common area washroom, leaving the student with absolutely no privacy!

Of course, the student was removed from the home and the Homestay Host was dropped from the Homestay program.

This of course is not a common misuse of respect and trust, but it does happen. I am not aware of any government policies (regulated) over this type of misuse at the time of publishing this book, but I, personally, would like to see some implemented. This type of unsuitable accommodation and any misuse of the system should be exposed and dealt with.

When it comes to renting your rooms, consider whether or not you would stay in the room yourself. If the answer is **no**, the room is not rentable space.

The Guest Room Essentials

- ❑ **Private** room with locking door or a lockable drawer or cupboard to store their valuables.

- ❑ **Neutral room color** is a good idea. Avoid child-like wallpaper, family or personal things, toys, etc. Let the Guest personalize the room since they may be staying for a length of time.

- ❑ **Window** to the exterior is essential for ventilation and daylight in all rooms. The window must open and be large enough to be used as a fire exit. (Check your local building codes for the minimum window size.)

- ❑ The **window coverings** should be in good condition (i.e. blinds that work or drapes that fit) and provide privacy.

- ❑ **Fully furnished** room includes all amenities (i.e. desk, lamps, full-size bed and bedding, wastebasket, etc.).

- ❑ **Bed** and the **mattress** should be comfortable, clean and in **near new condition**.

- ❑ **Bedding and blankets** go without saying. The Guest linen and bedding should be clean and in **near new condition**. It is easy to replace once it gets slightly worn out. Remember to add an extra blanket or two in the closet.

- ❑ **Clothing storage** should include a closet with hangers, and a dresser in good condition. Remember to provide enough space for storing luggage.

- ❑ **Desk and chair are** essential since, most Guests are here to advance in their studies. Make sure that desk and chair are a proper size to accommodate a computer with adequate working space, and are in good condition.

- ❑ **Internet access** is a must for a great Homestay Guest room. Most Guests will come with some type of computer. Internet connectivity is easily achieved by visiting your local electronic store where they can help you get started.

- ❑ **Bathroom** with a lock. Supply toilet paper and hand soap.

- ❑ **Laundry** access, including washing machine and dryer and laundry soap.

Recommended Extras for the Rooms

❑ **Climate Controls:** In many cases, your Guest will be from a different climate than yours and controlling their own heat helps them to adjust for colder months.

  – **Heaters** in rooms are a nice option, especially if you live in a colder climate. Use newer, safety-regulated heaters with an automatic shut-off.

  – **Electric blankets** are a nice touch if controlled heat is not an option. This way, you don't have to heat the whole house, which helps to keep heating costs down and also keeps everyone at their own comfort level.

  – Check that the rooms are not damp and drafty.

  – Guests should never have to complain about being cold in your home.

❑ **Microwave** and/or **Small Refrigerator** in room or nearby common area. (This is highly recommended if you are not providing full Homestay).

❑ **Kettle and teapot**, cups, etc. for tea or noodles is often appreciated. I recommend always using electrical appliances that have automatic shut-offs.

❑ **TV** in the Guest room is a nice option if a TV room is not close by. Since your Guest tends to spend a fair amount of time in their rooms, having a TV is a small comfort and a great tool for learning the language

❑ **Telephones** should be easily accessible along with up-to-date yellow pages directory. Explain your rules about phone use.

❑ **Additional Telephone Lines** are a great idea.

  – Some Homestay hosts choose to have a separate phone line installed for their Guest as it frees up your personal line.

  – In this hi-tech era, most Guests will purchase a cell phone if they are planning to stay for any considerable amount of time.

❑ For **Long Distance**, I would recommend that you have the phone company put a block on that line so no out-going long distance calls can be made except with a long distance calling card to ensure you are not stuck with unnecessary phone bills. Explain to the Guest where they can purchase Phone Cards.

❑ **Emergency Numbers** should be posted near the phone. Do not assume that numbers and procedures are the same in all countries. Having this information visibly posted can save a lot of valuable time in case of an emergency.

❑ **Side chair** – an extra chair in the room so the Guest does not always have to sit on the bed.

❑ **Tourist information** and local maps are important as sightseeing is always on the To-Do list for any out-of-town Guest. Be sure to include bus schedules and local phone books, as they will for sure be in need of one.

❑ **Safety Features** should include:

  – **Working smoke detectors** with **new batteries** (changed every spring and fall – with the clocks!)

  – A **proper Fire Exit** from working windows in each guest room.

  – **Fire Extinguisher** handy and in good working order can also be valuable in case of emergency. I recommend a fire extinguisher in or near the kitchen. No appliance should be used if it is known to be unsafe or questionable.

Guest Room Checklists

Here are a few more handy checklists so you can see if you are ready to begin! The * indicates the item is optional.

The Room

- ❑ Private room with door locks inside and be adequately spacious
- ❑ Working locking window, with window coverings that fit
- ❑ Clean carpeting/ flooring/mat
- ❑ Working smoke detector/inside room or outside near by door
- ❑ Electrical outlets (minimum two)
- ❑ Good clean bed and mattress/mattress cover
- ❑ Clean, newer bedding, linens and two pillows
- ❑ Extra blankets
- ❑ Desk/proper desk chair
- ❑ Proper clothing storage/dresser
- ❑ Clothing hangers (minimum 10)
- ❑ Book case/Book shelf
- ❑ Wall mirror
- ❑ Reading lamp/overhead room lighting/new light bulbs
- ❑ Waste paper basket and extra small garbage bags
- ❑ Laundry basket
- ❑ Nightlight/plant*
- ❑ Internet connection*
- ❑ Phone line *
- ❑ TV *
- ❑ Small tea pot and electric kettle *
- ❑ Glass and cup
- ❑ All emergency numbers clearly posted near phone/house rules
- ❑ Bus schedules and transit routes
- ❑ Brochures of special attractions in your area *
- ❑ Local maps showing parks, shopping malls, etc. and neighboring area

Bathrooms

- ☐ Easy access with a **locking** door
- ☐ Small waste paper basket with extra garbage bags
- ☐ Toilet paper (endless amounts)
- ☐ New soap (prefer liquid soap dispenser)
- ☐ Clean hand towels
- ☐ Clean small bath mat
- ☐ Properly fitting shower curtain
- ☐ Bath towels and face cloths in good condition (Some Guests will supply their own.) Please do not give your Guest your oldest or worn-out towels!
- ☐ First Aid kit
- ☐ Shampoos and conditioners * (Guests usually supply their own personal items and toiletries, but you should still have a supply.)
- ☐ Rotating schedule * (Bathrooms may be shared, but each Guest's privacy is to be respected at all times. A rotating schedule for bath and showers ensures that everyone gets hot water!)

My pet peeve – OLD SOAP!

There is nothing more unprofessional than used soap in a Guest bathroom. Never have a used bar of soap out when a new Guest arrives. Change the soap bar often, as it is very inexpensive. Even better, use liquid soap dispensers at the sink and in the shower!

Common Area or Family Room

- ☐ Inviting area and welcoming atmosphere
- ☐ TV with video and/or DVD players
- ☐ Games and playing cards
- ☐ Books of interest
- ☐ Blanket (throws)
- ☐ Proper and adequate sitting
- ☐ A good selection of movies on video or DVD
- ☐ Filtered water
- ☐ Keys to the front entry (Your Guest should be able to come and go as they please, unless they are very young. Use your discretion.)

Making the Right Connections

Finding the Homestay Schools and Organizations

The Phone Book

A great way to find the international schools in your area is to simply open your local phone book. You can phone the local schools and institutions and ask if they have a Homestay program in place.

❑ Phone and speak with the person in charge of the Homestay department (usually the Homestay Coordinator) to find out about their particular program and request that they mail you an application form. Develop a good relationship with the Homestay Coordinator, as they can be a valuable contact and resource.

❑ If you prefer, you can visit the school/agency and discuss their Homestay program with the coordinator and then register your home in person.

The World-Wide Web

The Internet also provides a wealth of information to get you going. Check the websites for the schools and/or institutions in your area and review the information about their Homestay program.

> Many homestay websites are set up for you to advertise your accommodation.

Often the website has an application form, which can be filled out and sent over the Web. Many Homestay websites, such as www.homestaycentral.com, are set up for you to advertise and promote your available accommodation so Guests and Students can find your Homestay.

The School District

Another method is to contact your local school district. They will likely have a Homestay program in place, or will assist you in finding the schools in the area that are hosting international students. Many international high school students study abroad and are housed in Homestay for their comfort and safety.

Check out the www.homestaycental.com discussion board/blog to post questions and answers and to find a school or agency in your area.

Homestay Agencies

Many international schools deal directly with agents. These are usually privately-owned agencies that aid in helping international students and or traveling visitors with their visa arrangements, school placement and find appropriate living arrangements including Homestays. Some agencies can be easily found on the Internet — look for one in your area.

Chamber of Commerce

Contact your local Chamber of Commerce. They can provide great information on tourism and homestay businesses in your area.

Where Else?

Homestay programs are found at most colleges, universities, private schools, and sports camps and even through local churches. Many agents and organization will advertise in local newspapers looking for hosts in their area. Of course, word-of-mouth is another great source for contacts.

Registering Your Homestay

When registering your Homestay with an agency, school, or on an Internet Site, an application form will need to be filled out. There will be many questions about your home and family that will need to be answered.

❑ Tell them about your family, interests and hobbies.

❑ Describe your home and the wonderful Guest accommodations you have available.

> I recommend that you submit one or two pictures of your home and family as wells as a picture of the Guest room. This little gesture goes a long way when first starting out.

❑ For the safety of the students, most schools and agencies require a criminal background check for each potential Host.

❑ Some schools and organizations may request the potential Host to provide a letter of reference.

❑ Your application will be followed by a home visit by a Homestay coordinator.

❑ Property appearance should be clean and tidy; both externally and internally Cleanliness is essential in all areas of the house used by your Guest, especially the bathroom. Cleanliness of the kitchen, and refrigerator as well as any area that food is stored or prepared is also extremely important.

How the agencies and or schools view your home and family is very important. Their goal is to provide, quality, safe Homestay to students, tourists, visiting professionals, etc. and to use their experience and knowledge.

You may or may not like what they have to say, but remember, their main concern is the well-being of the Guest. Their advice is important in managing a good Homestay, so TAKE WHATEVER STEPS necessary to comply with their guidelines and make your Homestay a wonderful place to live!

The Right Mix

Finding suitable matches between Homestay Hosts and Guests is important!

In most cases, the Homestay Hosts may choose to Host a female or male Guest in their home. Some companies will decide this for you, taking into consideration your living situation.

For example, if you have a teenage boy living at home, it may be inappropriate to place an international female student of similar age. A male student would likely make a better family match. The parents of these students usually prefer this as well.

You may find that a Guest is demanding over and above what is expected from you as a Host. If you feel that he/she is taking advantage of your hospitality, please remind them that this is a family home and not a hotel. Do not feel that you need to give in to any unreasonable request in fear of losing your Guest. This is not worth the mental and financial expense and may cause you to resent your Guest. This would be a good time to go over your Homestay Agreement.

Finding the right match between Hosts and Guests makes the experience more rewarding for everyone.

The next sections are examples of applications and questions that the schools and agencies may provide for host and guest. This will help you to understand the types of questions that will be asked by the coordinator in charge.

Please note: that these are example pages only and that every school/agency will have a different approach for interviewing Guests/Hosts.

Sample: Student/Guest Application for Homestay Program

Tell us about yourself

Family Name		First Name	
Date of Birth (DD/MM/YY)		Sex: ❑ Male ❑ Female	If under 18 years old, do you require a Guardian? ❑ Yes ❑ No
Father's Name		Mother's Name	
Home Address		Home Telephone	
		Fax	Email
Father's Cell/Work Telephone		Mother's Cell/Work Telephone	
Allergies or Health Concerns			
Emergency Contact Person		Emergency Phone	Relationship
Comments			

Tell us about your Homestay requirements

Start date (DD/MM/YY)		Number of weeks:	
Room Preference ❑ Single ❑ Shared ❑ Full-board ❑ Half-board	Will you live with: ❑ Young children ❑ Older children ❑ No children ❑ Don't care	Do you smoke? ❑ Yes ❑ No	Do you like animals? ❑ Yes ❑ No
		What are your hobbies?	
What are your favorite foods?			
Are there foods you do not eat?			
Do you have any special diet requests?			
Do you take medication? ❑ Yes ❑ No If yes, please describe:			
Do you suffer from allergies? ❑ Yes ❑ No If yes, please describe:			
Comments:			

Tell us about your School/Institute and Homestay Agent

Name of School/Work attending	Course start date	
Education Agent	Agent Phone	Agent Fax
Comments		

Tell us about your arrival and homestay agent

Arrival Date (DD/MM/YY)	Arrival Time	Flight Number
Do you require Airport Pickup? ❑ Yes ❑ No	How long is your stay?	
Comments		

Acceptance
I have read and agree to all the conditions of enrolment outlined above:

Full name	
Signature	Date

Conditions & Cancellation Policy (Sample only).

Please note that accommodation and airport pickup will not be confirmed until all fees are paid. Request for homestay accommodation must be received at least two weeks before student arrival. Accommodation booking is for minimum four weeks. Accommodation Placement Fee and Airport Pickup fee are not refundable. Full homestay fees are only refundable if cancellation received prior to 48 hours of arrival. Homestay fees will incur 50% Cancellation fee if notification received within 48 hours of arrival.

Sample: Host Family Application for Homestay Program

*Please complete the attached questionnaire only after
you have read the Guidelines for Host Families attached.*

Personal Details

Family Name	First Name
Home Address	Home Telephone
	Work Telephone
	Email
Nationality	Fax

Is English the only language commonly spoken in your family? ❑ Yes ❑ No
If no, what other languages are spoken:

Wife/Partner:		Husband/Partner:		Children living at home:
Age Group	Occupation	Age Group	Occupation	1. ❑ Male ❑ Female Age_____
❑ 20-35	❑ Part-time	❑ 20-35	❑ Part-time	2. ❑ Male ❑ Female Age_____
❑ 35-50	❑ Full-time	❑ 35-50	❑ Full-time	3. ❑ Male ❑ Female Age_____
❑ 50-65		❑ 50-65		4. ❑ Male ❑ Female Age_____
❑ 65+		❑ 65+		5. ❑ Male ❑ Female Age_____

Family Interests and Hobbies

House

❑ House	❑ Apartment	❑ Garden	#_____	Bedrooms
❑ Balcony	❑ Radio	❑ TV	#_____	Bathrooms
❑ Video	❑ Internet	❑ Central Heating	#_____	Showers
❑ Continuous Hot Water		❑ Pets *(Please list)*	#_____	Toilets

How far is it to the nearest Bus Stop/Public Transportation?

How far is it to the nearest Shopping facilities?

How long will the student take to journey to their college/university?

Comments

Rooms

Does each room have:

❑ Full size bed	❑ Wardrobe/Closet	❑ Chest of Drawers	❑ Single bed #_____
❑ Window	❑ Table/Desk	❑ Table Lamp	❑ Twin
❑ Lockable Drawer	❑ Chair	❑ Heating	(2 single beds) #_____
❑ Mirror	❑ TV		❑ Double bed #_____

Comments

Meal Arrangements

❑ Full-board (Three meals/day) ❑ Half-board (Breakfast/Evening meal) ❑ Bed & Breakfast ❑ Self-catering	What time do you usually have the evening meal?
	Are there any restrictions on the use of the kitchen or other rooms in the home?

Comments

Arrangements for Students/Guests

Will the guest have access to the following?

❑ Washing Machine	❑ Incoming Telephone calls?	❑ Long Distance
❑ Dryer	❑ Outgoing Telephone calls	
❑ Iron	❑ Kitchen for tea and snacks	

Do you offer Laundry Services	❑ Yes ❑ No	
Are students allowed to have visitors?	❑ Yes ❑ No	What times?
Do you have any extra charges to the students?	❑ Yes ❑ No	Please specify:

Comments

Host Family Requirements

Note: We understand that you may take holidays or stop accepting guests for periods of time. The information requested is for general planning purposes and does not indicate firm commitment to these times.

Please indicate your availability:	❑ All year	❑ Summer	❑ Christmas	❑ Easter
Please indicate the type of guests you wish to receive:	❑ Male	❑ Female	❑ Married Couples	❑ Unmarried Couples
Age Group:	❑ 11-16	❑ 16-30	❑ 30-50	❑ 50+
Can guest smoke in:	❑ Whole House	❑ Own Room	❑ Outside Only	❑ not at all
Can you provide special diets?	❑ Yes ❑ No	❑ Diabetic	❑ Vegetarian	❑ Other

Can you accept a guest with a physical handicap? ❑ Yes ❑ No

Do you accept guests from other organizations? ❑ Yes ❑ No

Comments

Payment Instructions

I wish to be paid by   ❑ Cheque   ❑ Directly to Bank Account

Home Photo

Please attach a photo of the house and the rooms available.

Acceptance

I have read the guidelines for Host Families and have understood and agree to all the conditions as described.

Signature	Date

FOR OFFICE USE ONLY

Host Family Ref #	Accepted ❑ Yes ❑ No	❑ 1st Inspection Rating	❑ 2nd Inspection Rating	Comments

Guidelines for Host Families

Welcoming Strangers

Both Hosts and Guests need to establish mutual respect from the beginning.

> Both Hosts and Guests need to establish mutual respect from the beginning

The Guests are coming to stay in your **home!** They should feel welcome and become easily at ease, but also should respect you, your property and your household's standards. It is a two-way street, and clarifying expectations from both sides goes a long way to smooth the Homestay experience.

Mutual respect is a foundation for building any relationship, whether it is short-term or long-term. I know of several occasions where the relationships developed so well that the whole family has been invited back to the Guest's home country (sometimes all-expenses paid).

Extras Go a Long Way

I find that a welcome gift left in the rooms for when they arrive is a one of the nicest welcomes for any tired and weary traveler. This is a common practice in most overseas countries.

A little memento from you could be a book on the visiting city, or maybe a "Welcome to Our Home" card with a nicely framed picture of your home or family. How about little wrapped chocolates on the pillow? Any such gesture will say welcome to our home. Small delightful things make a big difference in keeping your Guest at ease.

Orientation to Your Home

You are responsible for introducing your home to your Guest. I strongly recommend that you introduce the Guest to all members of the household as soon as possible.

Be aware that certain things that we take for granted could be very unfamiliar to an International Guest. It is important to ensure that your Guest knows how to use all the house facilities. Be patient with them and show them what to do by giving them an orientation to your home.

Explain your family daily routines, schedules, and expectations. Remember that the Guest's/student's assumptions may be quite different from yours – he/she may have no idea why something is important to you.

It is totally up to you what can be used and what your Guest cannot use in your home. Please use good judgment and check to make sure that they completely understand your directions.

You may wish to repeat the orientation again in a week or two and clarify any new questions that have come up.

❏ **Appliances:**   Some appliances work differently in other countries. You will want to make sure your Guest understands how to use them properly. If you are leaving a kettle or any small appliances in the Guest room, I strongly recommend that they have **an automatic shut-off**.

❏ **Filtered Water:**   This is essential and a must have. In many countries, tap water is not used for drinking and therefore most International Guests will only drink filtered water. Be sure to have lots of filtered water available for your Guests.

❏ **Kitchen:**   Discuss the meal times and show them the snacks available.

❏ **Bathroom:**   The bathroom can be the most puzzling area for many overseas Guests. Explain how things are done in your home regarding storage, towels, faucet operation, shower and curtain, drain, etc. Suggest removing hair from the drain, tile and floor area and disposing wrappers and so forth in the trashcan only, NOT the toilet. Ask your Guest to leave the bathroom clean and tidy after use.

❏ **Toilets:** When disposing of toilet paper, some Guests will use the garbage can instead of the toilet. Other Guests may assume that our plumbing can handle almost anything! This is something you need to go over with your Guest to save you from unexpected plumbing problems. Explain to your Guest what is acceptable and what is not. We have found that leaving a short friendly note in the bathroom helps.

❏ **Shower curtains:** These are not always found in overseas homes and consequently some water mess is common. Most Asian homes and European bathrooms are fully tiled with a drain in the floor. Many Guests are not used to containing water in a tub/shower alcove. You may need to explain the proper use of a shower curtain. Show them that it sits inside the tub area only.

❏ **Baths:** Some Guests will prefer a shower and may even feel that a bath is unhygienic.

❏ **Hot water:** Many homes vary in size, as do their water tanks! Inform your Guest that since there are more people living in the home, more water is being used and that hot water is limited. Pre-determine a time length for showering, so that there is enough hot water for everyone.

❏ **Telephone:** All new Guests will want to call home when they arrive. Explain how to use the telephone and how to call collect or with their prepaid phone cards. Today with technology as advanced as it is, most Guests come totally equipped with cell phones, computers and/or palm pilots to communicate with family and friends back home. Be sure to detail your long-distance policies.

❏ **Neighborhood** Please be sure that your Guest knows how to get to and from school/work/shopping/church. It is a good idea to spend the first two days familiarizing your Guest with all their needed destinations. Remember to give your new visitor an Emergency Card (see sample in "Keeping Them Safe") to carry with them before they leave your home for the first time.

❏ **Beds:** Some of the most common things can be very different for an overseas Guest. For example, sleeping in a typical Western bed. Some cultures sleep on top of the bedding or maybe sleep on a

firm mattress on the floor. They may not be familiar with sleeping between two sheets or may have a difficult time adjusting to the softness of a pillow-top mattress. Please take the time to explain how we bed down in our culture.

❑ **Laundry:** Many of your Guests have never had to wash their own laundry before. If your Guest will be washing their own laundry, you need to show them how this is done. They need to know that using the washing machine for two little items is not acceptable and to wait until they have a full load of Laundry — so helping them the first few times is advisable.

- Some Guests will want to wash their smaller items by hand, so a small washbowl or access to a laundry tub is helpful. It is a good idea to have a drying stand in the laundry room where they can hang some of their clean, wet clothes. This is typical in most overseas homes. An added benefit to a clothes hanger is that it saves on energy bills.

- I have found that posting washing and drying instructions in the laundry room at all times helps prevent any unexpected mishaps.

The Family Pet

Oh, how we love our pets! They go in the car with us. They share a chair with us. We kiss and cuddle them, and in some cases, they might even sleep with us! Unfortunately, most International Guests don't live with pets and are not accustomed to having them share the same couch with them.

> Some Guests are shocked if they see pets in the kitchen.

In some cultures, animals are considered unclean. A few religions even prohibit them from being touched. Your Guests may be uncomfortable with your pet living inside the home. So introduce "Fluffy" slowly and let them know he is harmless. Explain to your Guest that your pet is part of the family and that you will do your best to keep him at a distance.

At first, don't let Fluffy jump up or sniff your Guest. It's also a good idea not to allow pets in your Guest room at any time. Familiarize your Guest with the do's and don'ts of your pet.

Keep your pets away from the dinner table at mealtime and do not feed them in the same area as preparing food (at least until the Guest begins to feel comfortable with having a pet around).

In most cases, your Guests do get used to our furry housemates and may even become very fond of your pet.

Shows of Affection

In our culture we love to greet each other with warmth and affection. Hugging and kissing each other is not always considered acceptable in some cultures and the Guest may view this as inappropriate. As well, personal contact can be very frightening to some Guests.

When approaching your Guest, use good judgment and consideration. Use common sense when it comes to any type of affection and refrain from any kind of physical expression, or intimate conversations with your Guest at all times.

A warm kind smile that says hello and welcome to our home is all that is necessary when greeting and socializing with your Guest.

Food for Thought

Imagine arriving into a world where everything looks sounds and smells different from everything you have ever experienced before. Food is THE biggest cultural shock that I have found for most Guests.

> Food is
> THE biggest cultural shock
> for most Guests.

Tasting new and seemingly exotic dishes can be a challenge for both Host and Guest. Many people take years to acquire a taste for different foods; so don't take it personally if you find that your Guests are avoiding trying some of the foods that you have cooked. Don't expect them to like every meal that you have prepared.

However, it is important for them to try the different foods offered to them, so take the time to explain that they should try everything at least once. Of course, there will be foods that they just don't like or can't adapt to. Speak to them as often as possible to find out their likes and dislikes and to make the culinary transition as smooth as possible.

The North American style and preference for easy food and frozen dinners might be steak and potatoes to you, but to a new overseas visitor it can be a cultural and digestive shock. Raw vegetables, heavy type meats, and even fried potatoes may cause various digestive upsets. Some types of foods should be introduced gradually.

Another common issue can be that some Guests may refuse to eat certain foods for fear of gaining weight. Give them time. As long as healthy food choices are offered, most Guests will adjust.

> Let the Guest choose some familiar food.
>
> Rice is the most-served staple in the world.

Find the local ethnic food store in your area. Provide a detailed map, or take them there personally, and let the Guest choose some familiar foods. I recommend that you serve rice at least three to four times a week. Rice is the most commonly served staple in the world and will be a true comfort to your Guest, considering that everything around them is a culture adjustment. A supply of instant noodles and fruits on hand is also a good idea so they can make their own snacks from time to time. It is also important to explain to your Guest what foods are for snacks and what is not – or they may end up eating tonight's dinner!

If providing a full Homestay, another option is to take your new Guest to the supermarket soon after they arrive and allow them to point out some of their likes and dislikes. Although it may seem impossible to please all tastes, being open-minded and trying new things is important for both Host and Guest. This could save you disappointment (and money) when a meal is left untouched.

Remember that your Guest is here to learn the culture and your food is a big part of that experience! Let them know the food you prepare is part of the whole Homestay experience.

Common Misconceptions

The first year is always the most difficult, as you gain more experience in learning to deal with Guests in your home. Some people may decide that they are not able to handle the commitment and life style changes that come with running a Homestay.

> There have been times in my own Homestay experiences, when I tell myself "This is the last year that I'm doing this."
>
> But it doesn't take long to realize how lucky I am and I think about how other people are spending their time! (9-5 J.O.B.)

The important thing is to understand your strengths and weakness. Are you ready for the responsibilities that come with Hosting guests in your home?

Quitting that full-time job to try and establish your Homestay is something you need to give a lot of consideration. It is important to think about what you might be giving up, as well as what you are gaining. Can you deal with the fact that your guest might be here for the holiday seasons and family functions?

Now that you are working from home, your family and friends may have the misconception that you have all this extra time on your hands. They may assume you are always free for drop-in morning coffee or lunch dates and shopping. They may think that you must be able to take on extra activities such as volunteering at your local church and so on.

Those last minute plans may be a little more difficult to accept when you are responsible for cooking dinner that night and preparing lunches for the next day. The Saturday Night entertaining with friends might be a little less appealing. Do you really want to shop and prepare a large dinner after being a Host all week?

> Know when to take a break from Hosting so that you don't burn out!

I'm not saying that you won't have the time to socialize — just be well organized and ready for any unexpected situations that might come up. Remember, it is important to keep separate social time for your own family and friends as well as yourself.

Getting to Know Your Guest

As it would be impossible to try and know all personalities that travel abroad, here are a few little insights in or about some of your Guests:

- There is no such thing as a *Typical* International Guest.

- Most want to live in an environment where they can learn English and experience the culture. This opportunity to live the lifestyle up close is why they are traveling here in record numbers.

> "It is estimated that over one billion people are currently learning English worldwide."
>
> — British Council, English 2000 Project

- English improves much faster when living in a Homestay environment.

- Homestay can be one of the most rewarding experiences of their lifetime. Many of the Guests have never traveled or lived away from home before.

- I have found that it takes approximately three weeks for Guests and Hosts to adjust to their new situation.

- Many of the parents of younger foreign visitors encourage them to choose Homestay over living in a school residence, apartment, or a hotel; because they know the Guests will be staying in a safe home environment.

- Most go to bed much later then we do. It is not uncommon for them to stay up all night studying. The non-stop studying is a fact of life for many foreign students.

- In some parts of Asia, a common term: is "Pass at four, fail at five!" This means, you pass your school year with four hours of sleep a night or you fail with five hours of sleep a night.

- North Americans often look at life a bit differently. A quote from Dr. Phil, a famous American author and TV Host, when talking about his expectations for his own children:

> "I ask only two things from you. One is to get a good education and two, is to have a lot of fun in life, and in that order."
>
> — Dr. Phil

- Many international students are brought up with a different perspective:

> "One is that you get a good education and two, when you have accomplished that, get more education!"

- Post-secondary education is considered their greatest investment and the requirement for education standards are getting higher. This workload is a pretty tall order and can be over-challenging for them.

What's on Their Mind?

These intelligent minds that travel here from a foreign country are looking for something that's just not offered back home. The Guests choosing Homestay can sometimes bring their own challenges and misconceptions.

- Some come here and have unrealistic expectations about life away from home. They may assume families are like the images they see on television or in movies — wealthy and living the Hollywood dream in big beautiful houses with swimming pools, luxury cars and servants to cater to all their needs.

- Sometimes you have to remind them that you are not a servant, but a friend and a guide – their Homestay Host!

- Some Guests are quite amazed to see that families are all different races, or that they are sometimes single parents or perhaps childless couples.

- Guests can sometimes be shocked when they realize that both parents work and then can be quite busy in the evening with their children who are involved sports and after-school activities.

Talk about it!

I received a call one night from a Host parent that her new Guest was just not adjusting well and wanted to move from her homestay.

The Homestay parent stated that her Guest did not understand why the Homestay Host did not have a husband and why there were no children in the home.

He was very uncomfortable and felt that there was something wrong, so he wanted to move his Homestay. After some discussion and explanations, the Guest understood that his Homestay Host was single and recently divorced and was just looking for some company in her now empty house.

Things worked out great and they are now the best of friends. He stayed in her Homestay for the next three years and finished his studies. He still joins her occasionally for Sunday dinners.

- Money for the most part is not an issue and they arrive here with enough funds to live and educate themselves, usually for the next four years. That does not mean that the money is spent foolishly. Most are brought up to respect money, as it usually comes from a joint family account.

- Many of these Guests arrive and are accustomed to their own family's wealth. It is not uncommon for your new Guest to tell you he/she needs to buy a vehicle for transportation and to have them arrive home with a very expensive sports car.

The whole idea of Homestay is to live the culture, so do not make any drastic changes to accommodate their preferences. Be yourself!

Allowing for Cultural Differences

Try not to feel offended if your Guest does not say please and thank you as often as you feel they should. Different cultures express their feelings differently.

- If your Guest says something that comes across as impolite, they may have simply expressed it in the wrong way, due to their lack of English skills. Be patient, and be sure to take the time to clarify.

- Some uses of body language and odd gestures may seemingly be rude. Just ask them to explain and tell them how you feel. This will vary widely from country to country.

- One major stumbling block to communication is our cultural tendency to evaluate all behavior that is different from what we are used to.

Culture Shock

You may notice that your Guest may feel homesick when first arriving, or perhaps after the initial excitement of settling in wears off. This can make them anxious, confused and withdrawn. Trying to establish themselves in a new country and foreign surroundings can result in culture shock.

The Guest may feel homesick and the need for security and family. Your Guest may require a certain amount of settling in time. You may find that they will isolate themselves in their rooms for days on end without coming out to socialize or they sleep all day long.

Some younger Guests might be very emotionally upset and spend a great deal of time on the phone with a parent or a close friend.

If you find that your Guest is expressing odd behavior problems and having difficulty adapting to your home, try to keep to a regular routine (such as meal times). Let them know you are there for them.

Try to keep them involved with your family and your lifestyle routines such as regular meal times, recreational shopping, touristy things or other functions you may be involved in. Talk to them about their home and family.

We have found that this homesickness will pass with most students after the third week or so. But, if this continues for any longer length of time, it is advisable to inform the company or school coordinator involved because there may be a more serious issue.

The first three weeks are the hardest for everyone involved while everyone is getting to know each other.

Eva

When Eva was sent to us from China to study for a year, we were totally unprepared to understand what was happening with her.

She would come home from school every day and go to her room, close the door and sometimes we would hear her crying. I would try to comfort her and get her to join us for dinners but she would not communicate with us. As time went on things did improved and she came out of her shell and warmed up to our family.

We did not realize it at the time, but Eva was experiencing a severe case of cultural shock.

Language Arts

> Often reading is easier than speaking.
>
> Writing things down can often clarify your communication!

Homestay is the world's greatest classroom. Much of the purpose of Homestay is about language acquisition. This is one of the major selling points in the language industry. The ultimate gain is that the Guest is completely immersed in the English language while living in a Host home. Often reading is easier than speaking. Writing things down to can often clarify your communication!

International Guests feel they have better exposure to the language and to the culture in a Homestay. They would not get the same exposure if they were to move into an apartment or by living in a campus residence. This is their chance to develop the language at a faster pace from this cross-cultural experience. Living in a Homestay environment helps familiarize the Guest with the local area and helps improve their English by correcting grammar and pronunciation.

Leaning a new language can be difficult for anyone and can bring with it some of its own amusing moments. One of the most common problems is conversation.

Imagine coming to a new country and everyone around you is speaking a different language. This is a time when being a mime would come in handy!

> I don't know how many times my Guests and I have had to play hand charades with each other when trying to explain something that is not quite being understood by both me and our Guest.
>
> Whenever charades takes place, it can become quite comical with arms waving and fingers pointing. In the end, we usually understand and have a laugh!

We have a tendency to speak a little louder if we feel that the person we are talking to has limited English.

I'm sure we are all at fault for this at some point … maybe giving directions to a lost visitor or the guy driving the taxi or maybe when asking a stranger for directions — and because their appearance is of a different culture — we feel the need to **raise our voices** and do very comical hand charades. We **assume** they cannot converse in English, to find out later they were born and raised down the street from us and probably attended the same church.

The Homestay experience is the one of the most treasured aspects of learning a new language. Think about what they are hearing and seeing from their eyes. If we change our way of thinking, our habitual attitudes will change. Language and culture may be a hurdle, but it is the natural part of receiving international guests at your home. So remember:

❑ Speak only English when the Guest is present.

❑ Avoid speaking in broken English. Remember they will absorb what they hear and see and you want to be a good example.

❑ Speak clearly and a little slower than usual. Repeat and pause where necessary.

❑ Try to give all instructions in simple language and ask the Guest to tell you what he/she understood. Avoid asking, "Do you understand" as the answer will always be "Yes."

❏ Listen until they have finished speaking. North Americans usually place the most important points at the beginning of their speech. In some cultures it is the exact opposite, with background information given at the beginning.

❏ Watch for non-verbal cues. Pay close attention to the unspoken message – eye contact, arms and legs, silences, nods. Some say 80% of communication is non-verbal, especially at the beginning of the conversation. Tone of voice and facial expressions are important clues too.

❏ Remember that under conditions of high anxiety or fatigue, communication effectiveness decreases drastically. Do not overload your guest with information just when they have arrived. Give them a day or two to settle in.

❏ Know your own limitations and biases, and be open to cultural differences. Self-awareness and awareness of your own culture is essential.

❏ Younger children at home are great communicators! Not only do they enjoy having a new friend around, but also they love to teach them new things. Students do not feel intimidated by children and can pick up a lot of language skills from them.

This is a story I heard of two students from China who decided to live in a Homestay to improve their English.

Talking to Each Other

Everyone in the home spoke fluent English. Unfortunately there was very little communication between the family and the Guests.

The Hosts seemed to be very focused on their own lives. They spent very little, if any, time interacting with the students. Consequently, this led the students to only talk amongst themselves.

After two months of almost no communication from the Homestay family, and very little language advancement, the two boys decided to get an apartment. They did not wish to repeat their Homestay experience.

Lesson: Take the time to interact with your Guests and encourage them to speak only English in your family's presence.

Policies & Host Obligations

Guest Expectations

At the very least, your Guests expect to find a nice clean room, appropriate amenities and a friendly, helpful, happy family. If you are operating one of the full style Homestays, they expect a good breakfast, bag lunch and dinner with the family.

These are the usually the automatic expectations of all Homestay Guests and should be viewed as your Host obligations.

Younger Guests

Younger students come with more responsibilities and require more time. The biggest job is making sure they are safe. They are children and, at times, they will test their boundaries. Make it clear that they are expected to follow your house rules.

If you find that they are not abiding by the rules that are set, please contact the program coordinator **immediately** for the child's health and safety.

Most companies and/or organizations have their own policies on curfews and such when dealing with younger Guests. Check with them prior to your Guest arrival on their guidelines and expectations.

❑ General parental supervision is mandatory with younger Guests. Most teenagers are fairly restricted by their parents and may try to test their freedom with their Homestay family in the beginning.

❑ Curfews and excursion are mostly left up to your personal judgment.

❑ If you find that the Guest is defying you or being disrespectful, deal with it as soon as possible. It is advisable to contact the school or organization if it becomes more than you can handle.

Host Vacations

❑ **Your Vacation Plans:**   If the Homestay family has planned and booked a holiday, you need to let your Guest and organization know as soon as possible. Perhaps you would like to invite your new houseguest along. As a rule, the Guests are responsible to pay his or her own traveling expenses, as only room and food is covered under their Homestay fee.

❑ **Long-Distance Holidays:**   Some program polices do not allow you to travel out of the state or country with your Guest. Please make sure everything is properly approved before making any plans. If the Guest is under-age, (under 18 years) it is imperative that you have written permission from the legal guardian before venturing on any long distance holiday.

❑ **Check the Documents:**   If traveling with your Guest out of the country, be sure to review his or her visa or passport documents. You would not want to get into a situation that holds you up at customs and your much-anticipated flight is missed. This could be very costly for you and leave you in a situation with a stranded Guest.

House for Sale

I am sure this is rare, but if you decide to sell your home or move residence while you are Hosting, please let your Homestay Guest know well in advance so new arrangements can be made. It is also a good idea to notify the school or organization you are registered with as soon as possible.

House Rules

> Having House Rules in place **and in print** ... is usually the best way to start off a happier Homestay relationship.

Call them House Guidelines, Rules, Policies or Expectations — the **House Rules** generally consist of common-sense guidelines written in very clear, simple language. Having House Rules in place **and in print** and then discussing them with each new Guest in the beginning, is usually the best way to start off a happier Homestay relationship. Point out any family rules that are important to you and you wish to have followed.

❏ Put House Rules on paper and in a convenient location (i.e. their room, near the bathroom, etc.). This will act as a reminder!

❏ Discuss the House Rules within the first few day of your Guest's arrival. Go over them again after a week to review and make sure everything is understood.

❏ Ensure that there is a mutual understanding of such things as meal times, time deadlines for incoming calls in the evening, bringing unexpected guests home, curfews (if applicable), shut-down time to kitchen and laundry access, etc.

> Communication is the best form of problem solving!

The Homestay experience is a unique and valuable experience for an International Guest, but they must never lose sight of the fact that this is your home. You will set the standards and the rules that your visitors are required to respect and abide by for the duration of their stay.

Having posted **House Rules** will help to avoid any misunderstandings and having to solve any awkward conflicts. Communication is the best form of problem solving.

Setting the House Rules

When setting down the rules of the house, remember that many things that you find second nature and are everyday habits may seem strange to your Guest. How we live day-by-day without a second thought will not always be of the same significance to your Guest.

> To avoid things like growing unwanted science experiments, ask your Guests not leave dirty dishes and open food in their rooms.

Remember that your Guest will require time to adjust to this new culture and environment. Patience is a virtue, so be tolerant of differences and expect mistakes to be made.

Deal with problems and come to mutual understanding. If you find that your Guest will not abide by your house rules, then it is advisable to contact the school or organization and ask them to speak with your Guest.

Following is an example of the House Rules that we have used in our Homestay and developed over time. I have included a few extra ideas to give you options. Feel free to use what you wish and adjust them to fit your own needs and circumstances.

> All Rules should be based on mutual respect and human rights!

Our House Rules

Welcome to Our Home.
We hope you enjoy your stay with us.

These are the House Rules that we all follow.

Please feel free to ask questions if there is something that you do not understand.

**Remember this is a family home!
We all must do our part to help each other so that this is a great experience for everyone**

As a Homestay Guest

❑ Please **LOCK the entrance door at all times** coming and going and take your key with you, lock your bedroom window when you are not at home and <u>do not</u> let anyone use your key!

❑ Please remove your shoes at the entrance door.

❑ Call and let us know if you will be staying out for the night (so we don't worry).

❑ You are here to learn English. Please try to speak English when talking in the main parts of the home (your room is OK).

❑ Please talk to us if anything is bothering you. We will try to help solve the problem. (We can't help if you don't talk to us and we want your stay to be as pleasant as possible.)

Room Fees, etc.

❑ All Homestay fees are due on the date of your arrival and are due on the same day each month. If there is a problem concerning your fee, please let me know as soon as possible.

❑ If moving out, one month's notice is required in advance.

❑ If you are planning a trip away longer than a month, a fee of ½ month's rent is required to hold your room.

❑ There is a fee of $_____ (i.e. $50.00) if transportation is required to or from the airport.

In the Evening

- ❑ Complete phone calls by 10 p.m. No incoming calls after 10 p.m.

- ❑ In the evening, turn off lights when they are not in use, please close all doors softly.

- ❑ All visiting guests must leave by 11 p.m.

- ❑ Please keep your TV and music low in the evenings to show respect for the homeowner and other Guests.

Bathroom

- ❑ Keep your showers to 10 minutes or less, as hot water is limited.

- ❑ Last shower is no later than 10:30 p.m.

- ❑ Keep shower curtain inside tub at all times, so water does not run onto the floor.

- ❑ Pick up and hang your wet towels to dry.

- ❑ Our floors do not have drains. Please wipe all water mess from bathroom floors and counter before leaving the bathroom.

- ❑ Remove all loose hairs from the bottom of the sink, tub or floor, so the drain does not clog.

- ❑ Please color your hair, and paint your nails in bathroom area only. Be careful.

- ❑ TOILET PAPER ONLY in the toilet.

- ❑ Tampons and sanitary napkins are NOT put in the TOILET. Wrap them in tissue and place them in the wastepaper basket.

Dining and Kitchen

- ❑ Dinner is served at _____ o'clock (i.e. 6 o'clock) on most nights. Please let us know if you will be late or not attending dinner.

- ❑ Lunch consists of a sandwich and/or noodles, fruit and/or cookies and juice.

- ❑ If lunch is not needed you must tell me the night before.

- ❑ Kitchen is closed at 9 p.m.

- ❑ If you would like a snack or a cup of tea, please feel free to help yourself. Snacks and fruit are always available.

- ❑ Please limit food eating in your rooms. Use common sense. Food scraps may attract bugs or mice into your room.

- ❑ Clean up your kitchen mess if you have been preparing food. Wipe counter and put dishes into the dishwasher, etc.

Laundry Room

- ❑ Your laundry days are Monday, Wednesday and Saturday.
- ❑ Last Load is at 10:00 p.m.

- ❑ Please read all the instructions that are posted in the laundry room when doing your wash. Check for any changes.
- ❑ Clean up any mess.

Other Things

- ❑ There are always Other Things that are specific to each individual household
- ❑
- ❑
- ❑
- ❑
- ❑
- ❑
- ❑
- ❑
- ❑
- ❑
- ❑
- ❑
- ❑

ENJOY YOUR STAY!

Have a great time in our Country!
We wish you to have a wonderful learning and cultural experience.

Thank You from Your Host _____

The Business of Homestay

The secret of being a good host is being organized. Whether you are offering Homestay for one Guest or managing a small accommodation business, organization and consistency are necessary. Once you have made the decision to become a Homestay Host, there are practical steps to take to ensure you are giving your Homestay a good solid foundation.

Of course, there is no simple formula for launching your Homestay, as each one is as unique as its owner. This chapter will get you started and you can adapt as you become more familiar with your Homestay operation.

So get ready and get organized!

Homestay Agreement

It is always a good idea to have a Homestay Agreement printed and in place when the Guest arrives. A well-written agreement will avoid any misunderstandings and conflicts.

The agreement outlines what the Guest can expect from the Host family and also what the Host family expects from the Guest.

> A well-written agreement will avoid any misunderstandings and conflicts.

The agreement should clearly state the rules and expectations regarding the condition of the room when they arrive and when they leave. Make it clear when their homestay fee is due each month. The agreement should also clearly state expectations regarding giving notice when moving out.

A printed agreement avoids any confusion at the end of your Guest's stay. Go over the printed agreement with your Guest and make sure that he/she understands from the beginning.

Putting your Home to Work

With all this money being generated in the local economies, homeowners are opening up their homes to welcome this cultural exchange and opportunities provided by foreign visitors.

In fact, I often hear that many Homestay Hosts are earning more income as a Homestay Host than they could at a part-time or even some full-time jobs, AND they have flexibility! They can choose how many Guests they will Host and, for the most part, which periods of time they would have rooms for rent. Often, they can adjust their Homestay business to suit themselves each year!

Homestay can be flexible. Choose the style that works for you and the accommodation you have to offer. Most of the time, you can arrange your Homestay around your lifestyle. Maybe you only want to Host during the school year, so you have the summer holidays off. Most students return to their family homes during school holidays. A Homestay term can be as short as three weeks, or as long as a year or more.

YOU ARE THE BUSINESS and wear many hats. It is important for you to realize and be prepared for many roles, including:

– Housekeeper
– Chef
– Guide/Aid
– Grammar adviser
– Nurse
– Homestay Host

– Handyman
– Accountant
– Plumber
– Counselor
– Tour guide

Shopping and Finding Discounts

You are now a volume buyer and you will use more supplies then the average homeowner.

❑ Find wholesale suppliers for your bulk buying.

❑ Create a standard shopping list and bulk-buy once or twice a month, so you are not running to the store every day.

Location, Location, Location

In the same way that location is important in valuing any type of real estate, location can be a key factor in the decision the Guest will make on whether this is the right Homestay for them. Simple things, such as:

- What is the cost of the Homestay fee?
- What type of accommodation is it?
- How close is the nearest bus stop?
- How close is the nearest shopping mall?
- How long will it take to travel to school or work each day?

Most International Guests come from large, very active cities and they like to know that they can go out and explore their new surroundings with ease. They like to know that they can commute to and from school or work safely and in a reasonable amount of time.

You can look around your own community and gather the relevant information and provide your potential Guests with the following:

- Brochures of special attractions in your area
- Website of your city/town
- Bus schedules and transit routes
- Local maps showing parks, shopping malls, etc.; city maps showing the neighboring areas
- Guided tour of the local neighborhood

Banking & Accounts

It is a good idea to handle your Homestay fees and expenses properly using a separate bank and credit card accounts from your own common living expenses and personal savings. This way, you can see what and where the money is being spent each month and it will simplify your bookkeeping, especially when it comes to tax time. I recommend that you do the following:

❑ Set up a separate, checking bank account, accessible with your bank card, for all deposits and payments related to the Homestay.

- ❑ Set up a separate, savings bank account for 10% of all deposits. This is discussed further in the next section.

- ❑ Set up a separate credit card to be used only for expenses related to the Homestay. (Optional)*

- ❑ Set up online access to your accounts, so you can download your account transactions directly into accounting software. (If possible)

The Cookie JAR - Pay Yourself First!

Homestay can be an excellent way to earn extra income, but, as I have mentioned before, **do not rely on Homestay as your only source of income**.

> Put some of that hard-earned money away each month and **pay yourself first!** Why not? You earned it!

Like many types of small accommodation businesses, the cash flow is not always consistent. So manage this as any other home-based business, and prepare for the months that income is not generated.

So, I recommend that you put some of that hard-earned money away each month and **pay yourself first!**

Why not? You earned it!

Usually 10% of each deposit is a good amount to put aside for those months that your rooms are not generating income.

You may even find that, at the end of the year, the money you have saved has grown and you can contribute to that much-needed vacation or upgrade that older van you have been driving. Perhaps you just want to invest and save in a retirement fund.

Those choices are yours and WOW! It's nice to have options.

Keeping Records

> As this type of business grows,
> it needs to become
> more professionalized.

Simple bookkeeping is necessary when running a Homestay. It is essential, especially if you are housing more than one Guest in your home. A good bookkeeping method is one that anyone who can balance a cheque book, can quickly learn.

As this type of business grows, it needs to become more professional.

❑ Set up simple bookkeeping system to record the total income and expenses. Summarize all expenses from the bank account, credit card and cash receipts each month.

❑ Keep the bank account and credit card statements organized and summarize the monthly total for food, sundries, etc. each month.

❑ Keep all cash receipts related to Homestay in a separate filing system (even the old cardboard box). Each month, group the receipts (i.e. parking, gas, etc.) and summarize the total for each expense.

❑ Keep the utility, telephone and cable bills for the household organized. As a percentage is used for the Guest, you can usually write off that same percentage of the household expenses. Mortgage interest too! Find out what your country's tax allowances are.

❑ Remember, "Pay your taxes and you will stay out of trouble!" If you have summarized your expenses each month (or so), it will be fairly easy to summarize the 12 months into an annual summary.

❑ Be sure to keep good records each year and retain all of the records, receipts, etc. as long as necessary. Most governments require that you keep all records for at least five years. Be sure to find out what the tax requirements are for your country.

There are Business Worksheets following that you may copy or adjust for your own purposes.

Business Worksheets

Here are a few worksheets showing the basics. Of course, you can customize them as you choose. Remember that these are usually one-time purchases. Many people will already have many of these items (bedding, etc.) so the cost can be minimized. *Please note: All entries below are fictional and are for example purposes only.*

Start-up Costs – Worksheet

Bed/Mattress...$ 200
Desk/Chair 95
Wastepaper Basket, etc..15
Guest Towels 30
Bedding & Sheets...60
Internet Hook-up 50
Small TV 100
Electric Kettle 20
Lamp..20
Miscellaneous 25
Total Start-up Costs for One Guest Room ....$ **615**

Income Record

Guest Room Income
    Guest Room 1 (3 meals a day) ....$ 700
    Guest Room 2 (3 meals a day) 700
    Guest Room 3 (no meals) 450

Other Optional Income (when applicable)
    Airport Pick-up/Drop off...50
    Driving 20
    ESL tutoring 500
    Laundry 30
    Miscellaneous 10
Total Potential Monthly Income ....$ **2,460**

Operating Expenses Worksheet

For 3 guests (approximately)
    Food/Snacks ....$ 675
    Hydro..30
    Heating & Electricity (Home) 40
    Gas/Petroleum for Automobile 50
    Cleaning Materials...5
    Miscellaneous 15
    Cookie Jar..200
Total Monthly Operating Expenses ....$ **1,015**

Rents and Fees

Homestay Room Rates

Pricing your rooms depends on many different factors such as location, size of room available, and type of Homestay style offered. Another consideration is the extras such as ESL, driving to and from school, work, etc.

If you are receiving your guest from a school or agency, ask them if they have pricing guidelines already in place. Base the rate on:

> Remember, you want the Guest to leave happy so that he/she will tell others of your great Homestay.

- Current local rent market (check the other Homestay rates in your area)
- School policies
- Room and Home amenities
- Meals included/not included
- ESL Language Tutoring
- Location

Here are a few suggestions to keep in mind:

❑ Always be business-like when handling the rent so there is no misunderstanding by either Guest or Host.

❑ Most Homestay fees are paid on the day your Guest arrives for the month and are collected on the same day the following month.

❑ Sometimes the school and/or organizations will pay you directly.

❑ Charging a room deposit gives the Guest incentive to leave the room in good shape. Use common sense when it comes to returning deposits. (Note: Some schools and organizations do not allow deposits to be taken from students.)

❑ Keep financial dealings straightforward and consistent. A misunderstanding regarding finances can create havoc with your Guest-Host relationship that can cost you!

❑ Check your local area and find out what other Homestays are charging. Phone them – it's great for networking.

Security/Damage Deposit

This is something you need to consider from the beginning. Some Hosts do not ask for a damage deposit and some do. Only you can decide on this issue. Check with the organization or school that you are dealing with regarding their policy between Host and Guests. This could differ with each organization and type of Homestay accommodation offered.

Have in place an agreement between Guest and Host helps to build a commitment and make clear to the guest that his/her room is reserved and they are expected on a specific date agreed to. You may consider charging a security deposit for reservation and deduct the deposit from the first payment.

Charging for Extras

❑ **ESL or homework tutoring:** This service is in high demand with International Guests. However, only an individual who is properly certified in this field should charge for their services.

❑ **Laundry Services:** Access to your laundry facility is included in full Homestay fees. If you are offering a half or boarding home-style situation, you may choose to make arrangements for charging to do their laundry. Be sure to let your Guest know up front what the cost of your doing laundry for them is.

❑ **Airport Transportation:** Hosts can charge a minimal fee for airport transportation. If you are going to charge a fee for airport pick up or drop off, check with the Homestay coordinator. There may be a policy and they may have that fee already in place.

❑ **Private phone line:** If a separate phone line from the household is requested.

❑ **Transportation:** In most cases, you are not the chauffer. Guests are responsible for getting themselves to and from school, work and outside activities.

❑ **Moving:** This situation comes up every so often. Your Guest may have decided to move from your home and they have purchased many things for their new accommodation (e.g. table, chairs, bed, etc.). It is **not** your responsibility to move them. If you have the means (e.g. a truck) and want to help them move, discuss it beforehand and let them know that a fee will be charged.

Late Fees

It is not very common to have issues with late fees. However, if this situation does occur, then deal with it in a professional manner and ask the Guest for their outstanding Homestay fee. Also, remind your Guest that their fee is to be paid by a certain date each month.

If the situation cannot be resolved, then you can always speak with the coordinator or agency involved. This would be a good time to go over the written agreement if one is in place.

Moving In and Moving Out

After a short period of time, some Guests may wish to change their homestay family, move into school residence or move in with friends. Unlike most residential rentals, Homestay is a month-to-month agreement between the guest and host family.

All Guests should arrive to a clean and prepared room, but that does not always mean that they will depart that way! Be sure to use diplomacy and good judgment when dealing with your Guests. You will likely need a little flexibility in this area!

In a rare situation, a Guest will come to pay their Host on rent day and then inform the host that they will be moving out the next day, leaving the Host with no advance notice and no one to fill the room. (See the Homestay Agreement.)

Some Guests will come to view your accommodation before they decide to stay in your home, so be prepared to show your home often when a room is available.

What Should She Do?

One Homestay Host called to complain that the Guest, who had been with them for over four months, had just informed her Host that she would be moving out the next day, with no compensation to the Host.

Unfortunately, her student had not been placed in her home from an organization or school with a set policy regarding this situation. The Host did not have a Homestay Agreement in effect with the Guest when she had arrived.

In the end, the Host was not compensated and the Host was left discouraged and with a vacant Guest room.

Vacation Policies for Guests

Long-term Guests may return home during school vacations (e.g. Winter break, Spring break and summer holidays). Some students may attend summer school to obtain additional credits towards graduation. Decide ahead of time on your policies regarding vacation and holiday times.

❑ **Check the Policy:** If your Guests are from a school-type program, it will be wise to check with the Homestay coordinator before you make any arrangements with your Guest. The school may have their own policies in place and are not always happy if you change the rules.

❑ **Security Fee:** Most schools and organizations do have a policy in place for long-stay Guests who wish to go on a vacation while living in Homestay. The Guest is responsible for a portion of their Homestay fee if their vacation is longer than a two-week period. In most cases, ½ a month's rent for each month is required to secure their room while they are away. I recommend that all payments be collected in advance.

❑ **Holding a Room:** It is highly recommended that you charge your Guest a holding fee to hold their room. This prevents you from being in a situation where a new Guest is looking for accommodation and you have a room that you could have rented, in case the original Guest changes their mind.

❑ **Waiving the Fee:**   If a Guest would like to waive the Holding fee during the duration of their vacation, it is advisable that they remove all of their belongings from their Homestay. That way you have a room available to work for you, with the option for them to return if the room is still available.

❑ **Use Your Discretion:**   Nothing is written in stone! Maybe you would like to take a little time off from hosting. Maybe your Guest is someone you would love to see return and has been with you for a while and waving the fee could guarantee them to return. This is something that only you can decide.

Adjusting Your Room Rates

There are cases where you find that you are not keeping your room or rooms occupied. This could be for a number of reasons.

☒ You are not situated close enough to the amenities required by the Guest.

☒ The amenities that are close are inadequate for the Guest.

☒ The room is not quite set up for proper accommodation.

☒ The room is too small and not comfortable for a Guest staying long-term.

☒ Some Guests just cannot adjust to your lifestyle. Sometimes just a mix of cultures can cause unfortunate differences.

☒ The food is usually too different from what they are accustomed.

☒ Noise from small children.

☒ Pets in the home.

☒ Any, many or all of the above.

As a good Homestay Host, it is up to you to take an unbiased hard look at your Homestay and re-evaluate the situation, then make whatever changes are necessary to improve your accommodation.

Like any type of accommodation, the more central the location, the more expensive the room will be. If you were staying downtown New

York, it certainly would cost you a lot more for your accommodation than if you were living 30 miles outside of the city.

For example, if your Guest needs to pay to travel to get to work and/or school every day, this extra cost could be a deciding factor in whether your rooms are occupied or not. Everything is relevant.

Do you really need to adjust your fees?

Before you jump into this decision, be sure that it is worth it to you.

There are many Guests on a budget who would welcome the lower fee, since study/work is their primary purpose and cheap accommodation fits into their budget. So, before you jump into this decision – be sure that it's worth it to you.

Try to avoid a situation where it costs you money by over-compensating your guest. Being a Homestay needs to work for everyone involved.

Please Note: Some schools and organizations have set rules regarding setting the fees in order to avoid conflict with other Homestay Host fees in your area.

Legalities & Liabilities

Municipal Zoning Regulations

Because most Homestays only host one or two Guests at a time, they are rarely required to be licensed or inspected by government agencies.

However, even if there are not any specific polices or requirements, it is still a good idea to check all the zoning regulations for your town or municipality.

❑ Ensure your home meets all of the appropriate fire bylaws (fire extinguishers, number of smoke detectors, bedroom fire exit, etc.)

❑ Check that the bedrooms meet building and health requirements.

Local Laws

It is worth reminding the Guest that they must observe and abide by all local laws and regulations at all times. Always keep in mind that your Guest is in a different country and is here to learn a new language, a new culture, and he/she has chosen your country and your city from all others places in the world.

If the Guest has any questions about local laws or customs, they should come to you for clarification. Your Guest expects to enjoy his/her stay and to go back home with great lasting memories.

Insurance

While most companies and schools take great care in selecting your Guest, in most cases, they will hold no responsibility for damages or loss incurred to a family that can be attributed to your Guest. If loss or damage occurs, negotiations between the student and Homestay Host must resolve any problem.

It is essential to check with your insurance company for what, if any, liability insurance is in place for housing Guests in your home. Your

house insurance may not have automatic coverage for Guests. (**Check your policies!**)

❑ Most Homestay organizations require that you carry a certain amount of liability insurance, so find out about their requirements.

❑ Check with your insurance company (BEFORE any Guests arrive) and ensure that you have adequate **property insurance** in case any of your personal belongings suffer damage.

❑ Make sure that you have proper **liability insurance** coverage in place before your Guest arrives.

❑ Advise your Guest **against keeping** large amounts of money in their rooms, and recommend that all monies should be banked or locked in their suitcase. It is a measure of protection for both the Guest and Host.

Medical Insurance

All International Guests are required to carry proper medical insurance. You will want to check with Homestay coordinator to ensure this has been looked after before your Guest arrives.

❑ Find out what medical insurance is in place for the Guests and what the contact information is in case of sickness or injury.

❑ Have a doctor's name and phone number available in your area in case of Guest illness.

❑ Walk-in clinics are readily available in most areas. Make sure the number is placed in your Guest's room and on the emergency card you have supplied.

❑ If you are hosting a younger Guest that is in need of medical service, take the student to your own doctor or clinic, and contact the Homestay coordinator immediately!

❑ Ensure that your Guest's Travel Medical Insurance is in place whenever leaving the country of the Homestay (i.e. short holiday or day trip). Although it is the Guest's responsibility to secure the insurance, it is in your best interest to ensure that they have done so.

Traveling out of the Country

If planning a day trip out of the country with your Guest:

❑ Make sure that all visas, passports and other identification are in place.

❑ Make certain that you have notified the people in charge of the Homestay placement.

❑ Ensure that **Travel Medical Insurance** is current and up-to-date.

Keep Them Safe

Obligations and Responsibilities

Remember that all Homestay Hosts are expected to provide a safe and supportive environment. The Homestay or program coordinator has the right to remove a Guest immediately from the home if the situation is unsatisfactory.

Not meeting proper requirements and expectations include, but are not limited to: not properly feeding the Guest, sexual harassment, family arguments, drug and/or alcohol abuse, etc.

If any of these cases arise, the Homestay Coordinator can and will call for termination of the Host from the Homestay program and will notify proper authorities, if needed.

Feed Them Properly!

A young man came to me one day to complain that he wanted to move out of his Homestay after one week.

He complained that his Homestay Host was not feeding him enough food and that he was always hungry.

He was only allowed one egg for breakfast, one slice of bread and a water-only policy, no snacks were ever provided and the refrigerator was padlocked at all times.

Once, the guest had arrived 15 minutes late for dinner due to a missed bus, and all food was put away and no meal was supplied.

The Host mother claimed that she is "on a budget".

What nonsense! Feeding your Guests properly is an obligation!

Health and Safety

As with any industry, safety and health are important matters. Safety is always a concern when accommodating a Guest in your home — not only from the Guest's perspective, but for you and your family as well.

> Safety is always a concern when accommodating a Guest in your home...

❑ While you don't want to frighten your Guest, discuss the importance of locking doors, strangers and places to avoid. It is always a good idea to have your Guest notify you if they are bringing someone into your home.

❑ Make sure that all Guests know the evacuation exits from your home in case of a fire, and are shown what to do in case of an emergency.

❑ Equip all areas with smoke detectors, for your own safety as well as your Guests. Install at least one on each floor and better yet, one outside each bedroom.

❑ In all rooms, post 911 and other emergency numbers in clear view.

❑ Do not leave personal medicines in your Guest bathrooms. All medications should be removed or kept in a locked cabinet.

❑ Keep a first aid kit on hand at all times.

❑ Do not supply any medication to Guests other than over-the-counter products.

If you are hosting a younger Guest, please use your own judgment and common sense. Ask yourself: Would you allow your own child to walk off? Do they know what to do in case of an emergency? Can they find their way back home?

Guest Emergency Information

Just as important as letting them know the safety procedures, it is essential for you to have information about your Guest. A good Homestay Application form will also include information about the following items. Keep these forms organized and available if you need them.

It is important to know who to call in case of an emergency. Concern for the genuine well-being of your Guest is important. Remember that most organizations have a staff member to assist you in any emergency situation.

Your Guest should keep their medical insurance policy with them at all times, and provide the Homestay with a copy in case of any needed medical emergencies.

> Concern for the genuine well-being of your Guest is important.

In case of an emergency, such as an accident, a lost student or any other difficult situation, contact the agency, school or any other emergency numbers you have been given as soon as possible.

If your Guest is displaying any odd behavior that you feel is unsafe to you and your family, or even to him or her, I would suggest that you contact the agencies and/or school immediately.

Please be sure that there are answers to these questions:

❑ ENSURE YOU HAVE AN EMERGENCY CONTACT NAME & NUMBER FROM EACH GUEST!

❑ Do they have any medical conditions that may require emergency procedures?

❑ Find out if your Guest has allergies to anything (chicken, beef, fish, nuts, cats, dogs, dust, etc.). Find out what to do in case of an allergic reaction.

❑ Is there any medication that they may need administered in case of an emergency?

Emergency Card

Emergency Cards should be given out to each Guest upon their arrival and they should be carried at all times by the Guest while they are staying in your home. The card should list:

- ❑ Homestay Host's first and last name
- ❑ Homestay Host's phone number and address, cell number, etc.
- ❑ An emergency back-up phone number (e.g. neighbor, relative, etc.)
- ❑ Local fire department and police numbers
- ❑ Nearest hospital
- ❑ Doctor's number or nearby walk-in clinic number
- ❑ Poison control center
- ❑ Ambulance
- ❑ Agencies and/or school phone numbers

Sample Emergency Card for Guest

You may want to photocopy this or create your own Emergency Card for each **Guest to carry with them at all times.**

In Case of Emergency, please contact _____

Phone _____ Cell _____

Address_____

Alternate _____ Phone_____

In case of EMERGENCY CALL 911. If not urgent, call the following

Police _____ Fire _____

Hospital_____ Ambulance _____

Doctor _____ Walk-in Clinic _____

Poison Control _____ School _____

Homestay Agency/Contact & Phone: _____

Just in Case ...

Kyhung came to Canada from Korea to start her four-year study program at the local collage. The day after she had arrived, she decided to explore her new surroundings and go shopping. She had been left on her own, with no orientation, proper instructions or directions. While crossing a very busy intersection, a speeding driver hit her; the student was rushed and admitted to the nearest hospital.

With her English very limited, and no information about her or her Homestay and how to contact them, the hospital was very confused as how to handle the situation. The parents were finally contacted in Korea... they were UPSET and FAR AWAY.

Also, the Homestay Host did not have the girl's proper name, as many students will give themselves a non-registered English name while they are in the visiting country. The Hosts had a very difficult time locating her.

Keep in mind that this is not a common situation. However, these are things that can happen. We cannot stress enough how important it is to make sure everyone involved has a clear understanding of what to do and are prepared in case of an emergency or if the Guest is lost.

Marketing 101

Publicizing Your Home

Publicizing your home for attracting new tenants can be easier then you think. There are so many different ways to let people know that you have a room for rent. When advertising, be sure to list any extra features you have to offer.

❑ **Internet:** I have found that advertising your room and availabilities on the Internet is a valuable resource. There are many Web-hosting sites that offer this service for a small fee. Go Google!

❑ **Photos:** Include photos of your room, home, family, etc. and the price of your available accommodation. People looking for a Homestay in your area from anywhere on the globe can contact you if they are interested. This is a great way to attract that overseas visitor.

❑ **Personal webpage:** Another great way to market your homestay is to create a personalized webpage or website. This can be done fairly inexpensive today. Many people search the Web for their accommodations and what great exposure! For examples, see www.americanahomestay.com and www.torontohomestay.ca

❑ There are also Homestay sites that will **advertise your home** and the room available for you worldwide such as our website: www.homestaycentral.com

❑ **Local papers, Flyers:** Advertising in the local papers can reach those Guests already in your area, looking to relocate.

❑ **Agencies:** Registering with an agency is another excellent place to advertise your Homestay. They often gather detailed information and match an appropriate Guest.

❑ **Translations:**   Check out the local college and schools on-line and find out if they are dealing mostly with one particular country (such as China). Then, have someone write the ad in that language as well as English. This lets International Guests know that they are welcome.

❑ **Advertise and Advertise!**   Continuously spread the word that you operate a Homestay. Satisfied Guests will spread the word as well. Continuing your advertising and networking all year can help keep your room/rooms booked well in advance.

❑ **Yard sign:**   Room for Rent

❑ **Be clear!**   Use clear simple language when creating your advertisements.

Here is a simple but very affective ad that I found in the local paper:

> **ROOM AND BOARD/HOMESTAY**: ESL TEACHER'S HOME –
> Friendly clean, furnished with separate bath and kitchenette.
> Near College and Bus route. Meals optional. Available now 555-888-8888

Homestay – The Great Alternative

Randy and his family were new to Homestay. Since they had always rented out the lower part of the home, they thought it might be a good idea to share the downstairs instead of having to give it all up as a rented suite. Homestay seemed to be the answer.

They thought that they would like to try advertising on their own. From Randy's research, he found that there was numerous ways to do this.

First, he checked with the local Chamber of Commerce to see if he could advertise in their annual guide and/or booklet. He also contacted the nearby travel agencies and dropped off his cards for referrals.

Randy found that most of the colleges have bulletins boards — so up went the posting he had carefully written out.

Business Cards

Even when running a home-based business such as a Homestay, business cards are a valuable tool. They tell people that you are serious about what you do.

❑ **Business cards** are very inexpensive to make and print out using your computer. There are many pre-printed business card pages available at the local stationary stores. As well, many small print shops offer business cards for a minimal cost.

❑ **PASS IT ON!** Pass your business card out every time you get the chance. They are great to give to other Homestay Hosts, previous Guests, meetings you attend, schools and social networking.

Networking

There are many good reasons to develop a network of other Hosts:

❑ You will find that interacting with other Host families will be great support, both in giving you new ideas and someone else to compare experiences with.

❑ Just to call to discuss that odd situation that has just come up.

❑ Maybe buddy up with another Homestay family and go on outings.

❑ Make friends with other Host families for support.

❑ Get to know other good Homestays and Hosts – places you would be confident to recommend if you hear of someone needing a Homestay that you cannot provide.

❑ The school/agencies and the Homestay Coordinator will always be available to discuss any concerns you may have.

A Guest of mine asked if I could recommend a Homestay for a friend of hers. She was arriving from Mexico and planning to study here for one year.

My house was full ... but I did know of a great Host family that would love to have her stay in their home. It turned out to be a great year for the student and the Hosts!

Tips & Advice

From Years of Experience...

Be Open-Minded

Having an overseas Guest definitely means being open-minded! Both YOU and your Guest will be exposed to new ideas and new information, so you need to be patient and take the time needed to explain why things are done a certain way. Don't lose perspective of who they are and where they are from.

Some Host families try to mold their Guest into their world. If you are expecting your Guest to always think and act the same way you do, it may be a sign that Hosting may not be for you.

How to Keep Good Tenants

Homestay Hosts should sell themselves. Being a good Homestay Host sometimes means going that extra mile and doing enjoyable things that keep your Guest happy. Perhaps you can invite them to partake in a family movie or an outing to the shopping mall.

> Being a good Host means smoothing the process to ensure that your Guests are comfortable and satisfied. Those "little extras" go a long way!

Some Guests might seem to need a little more than others. Some will not want to intrude on your lifestyle. Let your Guest know that you are there to help and to answer any questions they may have. Remember that almost everything is new to them. Take the time to smile and communicate with your Guest daily.

Keep in mind that while you want your Guest to feel welcome, you also can't give in to every situation either. Consider each request, but do not feel that you have to give in to all demands. However, if the request is reasonable and/or relatively easy to do, go ahead!

For example, suppose your Guest complains about the lighting in his/her room and state that they are finding it difficult to read/study. **Don't cheap out** for the cost of a brighter lamp. Adding one more light should not be an issue. The Homestay Host should happily replace or add a light rather than brushing off the request. Do not make your Guest feel like an intruder or feel unwanted. The chance of losing your Guest far outweighs the cost of replacing the lamp.

Little Extras That Go a Long Way

Being a good Host means smoothing the process to ensure that your Guests are comfortable and satisfied.

Getting Ready For Your Guest

Your attention to a few details before the arrival of your Guests will help his/her transition to a new life:

❑ Write a letter to your guest. Describe your home, family, pets, lifestyle, and your neighborhood. Include photos of your family and home, as well as pictures, maps, etc. Perhaps even send a short, friendly family video.

❑ Read about the history and culture of your Guest's country of origin.

❑ Purchase a bilingual dictionary to help you communicate during those first few awkward weeks.

A Basket of Fruit and Maybe a Cup of Noodles?

Leaving out some easy access snacks is always a good idea. Snacks can be simple, such as tea, juice, instant noodles, toast, fruit, etc. Though most Guests are responsible for their own extra snacking items, it's good for them to know that something is there if they have missed a meal or just need a late-night snack.

Prepare Your Guest's Room

Ensure that your Guest room is functional, comfortable and inviting. On arrival day, a small selection of snacks and beverages placed in the room may be welcome, as your Guest may wake up hungry during the night. His/her internal clock will take a couple of days to adjust.

Coupon Basket (Great Tip!)

One Host told us that she keeps all incoming coupons in a basket for her Guest. Keep the 2-for-1 on a new restaurant that might have opened in the local area or specials on movie rentals, tourist attractions … anything that may be of some interest to your Guest. It gives them something new to try and explore in their new neighborhood.

Hot Water

Since a shower usually requires less water than a full bath, you might want to offer a *Showers only* policy. Short showers (10 minutes or less) do not take up much time or hot water and also frees up bathroom time for all household members.

Explain to your Guest that there are more people living in the house and that the hot water supply is limited. I have never found this to be a problem. However, keep in mind that there may be odd Guest who, no matter how many times you remind them, will take that dreaded 2 a.m. shower anyway.

Comfort for the Soul

Baking is always a comforting delight in any culture. Why not surprise your family and Guest with warm banana bread, cookies or muffins from time to time? Any International Guest will love the unexpected surprise when they have been in their rooms studying so diligently or returning from a long day of sightseeing. Guest and family always look forward to this little touch of delight. Check out our recipe book from seasoned Homestay Hosts for some great ideas!

Saturday Night at the Movies

Why not try Saturday movie nights? This is a ritual at our house. We all meet in the family room after dinner with a good movie, warm fire and popcorn. Guests and family alike look forward to an evening of entertainment and good fun. It's a great way to make your Guest feel at home.

Happy Birthday to You!

Unforgettable memories! I always try to find out from my Guest when his/her birthday is and mark it on our calendar. We always take the time to have cake and a card; and serve their favorite meal. Nothing says "we are glad you are here" as much as a celebrated home-away-from-home dinner party. What a great way to make them feel at home!

Memories

Remember to use the camera! Don't forget to add all photos to your memories Guest book. Place it in your common area. All your Guests will love to look through it time and time again.

Conversations with Hosts

Something From Everyone!

This chapter was probably the most fun to write! Just being able to come together with fellow Hosts and share our stories: some stories are very funny, some a little beyond belief, and some that are just great memories (the good, the bad and the ugly!) We have dedicated this chapter to all Homestay Hosts who have their own unique story to share.

Of course, after you have been a Homestay Host for a while you will begin to get to know other Hosts. I encourage and highly recommend building your circle of Host's friendships. It's a way of being in touch and comparing any surprising circumstances that may come up.

Communicate! Communicate! Communicate!

Communication can be a fun challenge! Charades and language dictionaries are necessary! Patience will be rewarded with understanding!

The Rush

One Host loved to tell the story about her Guest who had not been living with them for very long.

As they were preparing to get her off to school, her Homestay Host exclaimed to her that it was getting late and they needed to rush.

The girl looked at her a bit strange and went into her room only to reappear with a jar of odd smelling ointment.

With a little bit of patience and the two of them playing charades, the Host finally understood that her Guest had thought she meant "rash" and was offering to help.

Homestay is an education for all of us!

The Unexpected!

Anyone that has raised a teenager knows that sometimes-difficult circumstances do happen. When teenagers are involved, you may come across a situation where the boundaries get crossed. This is not often, but never-the-less, **where there are raging hormones involved, common sense can be left behind.**

The Boyfriend

One night, our new Homestay Guest, 17-year-old Anna of one month, asked us at dinner if her friend could come over and stay the night, to help her with her research paper. Anna was a quiet student and seemed very serious about her studies. Since we had to go out in the evening for a short time we felt the company for her was a great idea. We allow the Guests to have a friend stay the night from time to time. It helps them feel more comfortable in our home.

When we arrived home from our evening the house was quiet and we just assumed that Anna and her friend had settled in for the night.

Oh yes! They had settled in quite nicely. The next morning, as we are preparing for our busy day, getting kids ready for school, etc., I was shuffling through the house and hurrying down the stairs half dressed - half pajamas, when I ran smack into a 6 ft. bare-chested young man exiting my washroom.

In shock, a little confused, all I could think to say at that moment was "WHERE'S ANNA?" At that moment, my two impressionable, young children arrived at my side wanting to see who had joined them for the usual morning rush.

My eight-year-old, whose room is directly above our Guest room, verified that they must be "best friends" because she had heard them "playing around" last night! That could only come from the mouths of babes!

I sent the boy on his way and explained to Anna that I felt she had taken advantage of our kindness, as I knew that she would never have attempted such a thing in her parent's home.

The problem was solved never to happen again and four months later Anna moved into her own apartment. We still keep in touch.

Unexpected and unwanted situations will come up. Dealing with them in a firm manner is what I have found to be the best approach. Remember that this is your home and if there is something that is totally unacceptable in your home then make it perfectly clear who is the adult!

Smile! You're on Candid Camera

We all have seen the tourist with the camera around their necks, taking picture after picture with endless amounts of film. Nothing is spared when these camera-crazy tourists are around. Today's digital cameras mean even more pictures!

Say Cheese!

Ken and Sharon found hosting to be the perfect balance to their busy life. So when the local college asked if they would like to Host two girls from Japan for the coming school year, they happily agreed.

Sharon remembers one weekend working around the house with her husband. Steve was helping with washing the dishes, folding the laundry and vacuuming the floors. They did not expect this to be so entertaining to the two Japanese students.

The girls were giggling away, following Ken around the house as he cleaned and wiped down bathrooms and later preceded to make us all lunch. They snapped picture after picture. They could not wait to tell their family and friends back home. Who would think that the man of the house would do all of those things? Where they come from, men never helped the women around the home.

This is a very common occurrence with some visiting International Guests. Most Homestays that have hosted for a long period of time can recount a similar story.

So smile — you're on candid camera! You may as well get used to it!

When in Rome ...

Hosting International Guests is truly a learning experience for both cultures and everyday common things can be incredibly different across the waters. Don't assume your Guest has the same common-knowledge we do – some things should be demonstrated and discussed at the initial orientation!

Sleeping on the Floor

This is a story that came to us from Darcy R, but I am sure it happens often...

She received a call one day from a local program that was in desperate need of a Homestay for a group of Japanese students that were arriving later that week. The original Homestay had cancelled out at the last moment and did she have space to take a 16-year-old boy.

Having the space available, we agreed to welcome this boy into our home for his stay in Canada. In the beginning everything seemed to go as planned. We found him to be a very polite and quiet Guest, and the limited English was something we worked through. Everything was working out great.

Very late one evening, I needed to talk with the Guest about an early trip he was going on in the morning. I reluctantly disturbed him and knocked on the door to his room. Half awake, he came to his bedroom door and I noticed that all the bedding was on the floor made into a nest bed.

A little stunned, I asked if everything was okay. It was fine, he replied. So, still a bit confused, I asked why the bedding was on the floor. A little embarrassed, he told me that back home his bed is on the floor, the traditional way of his country, and he had never really slept in this style of bed.

Not to sure what to do at that point, I decided to leave it alone and found more blankets for him to pad the hard floor. The next day I showed him how our culture sleeps in a bed, and how we sleep between the sheets, but left it up to him on what way he wanted to bed down for the night. We also let him know that it was okay with us whatever he decided to do.

Gifts – Shows of Appreciation

Many a Homestay Host has experienced the little trinkets and souvenirs that arrive for them with their new excited Guests saying thank you for inviting me into your home. But one story stands out about a very thankful family …

The gift that just kept on giving

Not being Homestay hosts for very long, Brian and Terry love to tell the story of the surprise gift that landed on their door one day from a very thankful Homestay Guest and the much appreciated family for taking such great care of their 17-year-old boy for eight months.

José from Mexico had just said his good-byes two weeks before, when a call came from the immigration office that a parcel had arrived for them, but it must stay in quarantine for several days and could they please come down and fill out the appropriate paperwork.

A bit confused, they headed down to immigration only to find out that they had graciously inherited a new pet from their overly thankful Homestay Guest. Yes! A happy wrinkly puppy sat waiting for this family to take it home and love and care for it for the rest of its (waggy-tail) life to remember their time with José.

All they needed to do was fill out the necessary paper work. I am sure and with all expenses paid by the overly grateful Mexican family, you would think that this very rare and expensive purebred would be a welcome surprise for most.

The first month was great with the new member of the family the kids loved him and mom and dad seem to enjoy the funny little new addition to the family. But as time went on they became to notice that their new little friend was not doing so well. So off to the vet they go …

To make a long story short, the new friend became a very costly gift. Being such a rare breed, he was prone to many types of infections and he developed several different health problems. With many expensive trips to the vet that required numerous essential surgeries, this family was not prepared for such a financial burden.

I am sure that the grateful Mexican family had no idea what kind of pressure they had placed on Brian and Terry. This gift was a well-intended loving expression of their appreciation … BUT …

What's Next

For some, Homestay develops into much more – a way of life!

Rita's Nest, B&B

Rita started hosting her Homestay slowly by starting out with one student. Over time, she found that she could accommodate two or three guests at once. Rita eventually realized that she and her husband really enjoyed hosting Guests in their home and decided to take it to the next level.

Rita changed her Homestay business into a **Full-time Executive B&B** where her guests are often traveling professionals and business executives. Many of her guests are in town for an overnight business meeting. Others may be attending a training seminar that requires them to be in town for a week or two.

The nightly fees are much higher than what is reasonable for a Homestay Guest, as is the Guest turn-over. However, Rita feels that the older, more sophisticated clients that stay at her B&B suits her style because she loves to cook, entertain and decorate.

In the off-season when business slow, Rita does admit that she welcomes having a student for a semester or two. That is one of the wonderful things about Hosting in your home – you can take breaks when needed and work the Homestay to suit your lifestyle.

We asked Rita what she thinks is the most important rule to live by, as a Homestay Host?

"Be consistent about everything you do in running your Homestay. A lot of my guests come from word-of-mouth. I am consistent about serving dinner on time and tidying up the house so that it is pleasant for everyone. I also take the time each day to have conversations with my Guests and just share the day's stories."

"I know these are the things that make my B&B and Homestay as successful as it is today."

Thanks Rita!

The Yin and Yang of Homestay

I recall a story of a Host family that had just received their first Guest and within 20 minutes of the guest arriving he had a severe allergic reaction due to the family pet in the home. He was then rushed to the nearest hospital for treatment. He went straight from there to a new Homestay. This was a very distressing introduction to the Homestay experience for both Guest and Host.

Every Homestay Host has a special story regarding a guest or two. Chris and Lee of Boundary Bay, B.C., have been Homestay Hosts for many years and have seen many Guests come and go. But not Alberto from Mexico, he stayed for seven years! This student remained in their home right through high school and went on to University. By then he was genuinely one of the family.

Share Your Homestay Stories

We would love to hear your interesting Homestay stories! Visit our discussion board/blog at www.homestaycentral.com/blog

Saying Good-Bye — Ciao!

Saying good-bye to a new friend can be hard ... so don't forget to exchange those email addresses! Now it is your time to sit back, put your feet up, take a deep breath and reminisce. Enjoy the moment!

Until you have Hosted an International Guest, you won't really know if this lifestyle is for you. Once you have Hosted, we trust that you and your family will have experienced something memorable or even a little magical.

Learn from any mistakes, if any, and prepare to open up your home for your next new visitor to the world of Hosting International Guests.

Homestay FAQs

Frequently Asked Questions

Where can I get more information and help?

Homestay Coordinators – at the school and agencies – are there for your support! They are selected for their people skills, organization and educational backgrounds. They are genuinely dedicated to the well being of the Guest and Host. They will answer questions, direct you to references, and help with solving problems.

There is also a great website discussion board/blog where you can post any questions you may have and advertise your available accommodations at

<u>www.homestaycentral.com</u>

How do I get started?

Make sure to evaluate your lifestyle first. Answer the 10-question quiz on page 15 in this book. Contact your local international schools and other organizations and have them send you their application forms. Fill out all material, then contact and follow up on your application with the coordinator in charge. It is always a good idea to keep in contact with the organization that you are dealing with and establish a professional relationship.

Is Homestay only for students?

No. Homestay Guests can range from working professionals, students, and visiting travelers to whole families.

Should I be concerned about the Guests that I am letting into my home?

International Guests must go through a very extensive visa and security process before arriving in your country.

What is the difference between Homestay and Bed & Breakfast?

Most Bed & Breakfast establishments offer a one- or two-night stay for their Guest, so a personal relationship is never really developed between the Host and Guest. A full breakfast is served in the morning and that is, in most cases, the only meal included in their stay.

Homestay Guests are here for a greater length of time and in most cases develop a relationship with the homeowner. Depending on what type of Homestay style you choose, many of your Guests will spend morning and evening meals with you and your family.

Do I need to be home in the evenings?

This question is answered based on what style of Homestay you are running and the age of your Guest/student. If the agreement includes dinner, then dinner should be provided. If you have a young Guest, they should accompany you and not be left home alone in the evenings.

Is it necessary that I be home for their arrival and departure?

Yes! Hosting is just that! You are the Host and need to be present when a new Guest arrives as well as when they depart. Welcoming and proper orientation to your home is required. The Homestay Coordinator will inform the Host family of arrival information.

In most cases, the Coordinator will take the opportunity to become acquainted with the Guest/student by meeting him/her at the airport. Then, after completing some preliminary paperwork at the agency/school office, the Coordinator will deliver the Guest to your home. This provides the Coordinator and the Guest with the opportunity to become acquainted.

Should I allow my Guest to bring friends home?

From time-to-time your Guest/student will bring a visitor home with them. Use your own discretion about the type and frequency of visitors. Make clear rules about when Guests can bring friends, where they should entertain them and what time their visitors should leave.

When and how do I get paid?

A Homestay fee usually starts and is paid on the day that they arrive. This fee is paid on that same date every month. Your Guest may pay you directly. Check with the school or agency regarding their policies. Some agencies/schools handle the fee process and pay the Homestay monthly.

Should I allow my Guest to use my telephone?

Most Guests will purchase a cell phone if they are planning to stay for any considerable amount of time.

If they do not have a cell phone, you may wish to get a separate phone line installed for your guests (Optional). This frees up your personal line. It also frees you from taking messages for them all the time.

What about long-distance telephone calls?

When they first arrive, most Guests will need to call home. This should definitely be allowed and encouraged. Perhaps you can welcome them with an inexpensive long-distance calling card and let them know where to find more in the future.

I would recommend that you have the phone company put a block on all phone line so no out-going long-distance calls can be made, except with a long-distance calling card. It also avoids the situation of you being stuck with unnecessary phone bills.

My Guest will not eat the food that I PREPARE.

Food can be an issue! We all have an attachment to Mom's cooking. Almost everything you serve is going to be new to your Guest. Some Guests do not want to try new and different foods, or else want to eat only their own foods. They are here to live our culture and mealtime is part of that experience. You may find that some Guests will eat very little in the beginning for fear of gaining weight.

Try having a culture night every once in a while and prepare foods that they are accustomed to. This will give them a dinner to look forward to and expand your cooking capabilities as well! Find out what is a main staple in their home and have it on hand (e.g. rice, Kim-Chi, limes, etc.).

My personal food supply keeps disappearing!

Even though it's important to make your Guest feel at home, you don't want them eating tomorrow night's dinner. There is no reason for your Guest to take things without your knowledge or to misuse their freedom.

Let them know that if they are hungry they are welcome to help themselves to the snacks, juice and fruit that you have provided. Show your Guest where snacks can be found in the kitchen.

What should I do when my Guest seems to be breaking our house rules?

If you find that the house rules are being totally ignored, then speak with your Guest and let them know how you are feeling. The lack of respect for you and your home is totally unacceptable. If this does not solve the problem, then phone the agency or school involved.

After they are notified, they will (in most cases) be happy to speak with your Guest. As well, we sometimes need to look at ourselves and consider if we have reasonable expectations. This is a good time to go over your house rules with the coordinator and see if the rules are too rigid or too lax. In any case, the problem can usually be worked out.

My Guests are entering our private spaces (e.g. bedrooms/offices). Is this acceptable?

Privacy is an essential element when several people live together. It is important that Homestay Host make it clear to the Guest that there are areas of the home that they should not enter. In most cases, these areas are the bedrooms of each family member. A home office or a garage workshop may also require this definition.

Is my Guest responsible to clean their room?

Yes. Some Guests may not be used to tidying their room or making their beds. Explain to them how this is done. Some Hosts prefer to clean their guestrooms. Have a regular time for cleaning and inform your Guest in advance.

What can I do if my Guest is not blending with our family?

This is not a common problem, but can happen. Sometime the chemistry is just not there. Speak with your school coordinator to see if there is something that could be resolved. It may be just a cultural learning curve for both of you. If this does not work, then talk with the student and let them know that you feel they would be happier living in a different Homestay. In most cases, a change is all it takes.

Should I have locks on the Guest rooms?

Yes! Unless you are hosting a very young student, I highly recommend that the Guest have the option of locking his/her door. This gives them the sense of privacy and independence. They trust their Host, but they may feel more comfortable with this option. It also discourages young children from entering the room or any unexpected visits from pets.

> I always let my Guest know well in advance if I need to enter their room for vacuuming or any other household chores.

My family is planning a full day out at a local amusement park. We would love to invite our Homestay student, but feel this could become quite costly. Are we responsible to fund their activities?

You may wish to plan an activity (such as a visit to an amusement park, swimming pool, skating and so on) with a cost involved. In most cases, it is the responsibility of the Guest to pay for any outside activity. This should be mentioned in advanced so everyone is prepared.

Of course, a Full-Homestay Host is responsible for making sure that their Guest is fed the appropriate meals. If the Guest is normally included for the family dinner, then you must keep the responsibility when dining out for dinner. Don't dine out with your family and bag a lunch for your Guest – it is totally unacceptable! However, if the Guest does not attend the activity, you must provide a meal at home with simple clear instructions.

Our family has a booked holiday. Do I need to find my Guest different Homestay, or leave them home alone?

If the family will be away overnight during the Guest/student's stay, please let your Guest know well in advance. As well, the family will make arrangements for a responsible adult to be left in charge. Notify the program coordinator of your plans and leave a phone number where you can be reached.

What do we do if there is a family argument?

We are all human, and these unexpected situations seem to happen at the most inappropriate times. If an argument between family members breaks out please assure your guests that everything is okay, and apologize if they felt frightened in anyway. If this is an on-going issue in your home, I do not recommend that you Host Guests. This is not what any visitor needs to witness! Remember, if your lifestyle is unsettling, so will be the experience be of the Guests.

My Guest has moved on with no forwarding address. What should I do with the mail that has arrived?

A Host may not destroy mail addressed to a previous guest. On the envelope, draw a single line through the name and address and write "Not at this address." Put the mail in a mailbox and the post office will return it to the sender.

I seem to be having difficulties with conversing and understanding my Guest.

Most Guests will have studied their host country language before arrival. However, books do not prepare them for daily language conversation. As a Host you may need to, on occasion, seek out help from someone fluent in your Guest's language. Look for support from the school or organization. I have found that writing out your question to the Guest works best in many cases.

How much of myself should I share with my Guests?

You are the Host. So helpfulness, kindness and genuine hospitality are what are required of you as a Homestay Host. Do not share your personal problems and any type of family disputes with your Guests. Do not burden your Guest with your personal problems, just as you should not get involved in their personal or family issues.

Recipes from Hosts

Food! Oh, wonderful food! It brings people together!

> Food!
> Oh, wonderful food!
> It brings people together!

Even with new and delightful dishes, the Homestay Host and Guest can find mealtime to be very difficult in the beginning. Just as you may find raw tuna a little unusual, pulling out a pound of the very best ground beef and turning into hamburgers can be disturbing to many an overseas visitor.

We would like to share with you some Homestay dishes that were sent to us from experienced Homestay Hosts. Ethnic shopping and cooking is like a passport to exotic lands. The aromas, vibrant colors, textures and flavors are worth exploring.

Since it can be very difficult to please all taste buds, here are some of our favorite delicious, taste-tasted recipes that I am sure everyone can enjoy. Go ahead, take a look at what Homestay Hosts are cooking up!

Western Wonders

Canadian Bacon Pizzas

Sent to us from Larry E. & Leah S. of Coquitlam, B.C.

¼ cup	mayonnaise or salad dressing
½ tsp	dried thyme, crushed; diced basil, crushed, *or* dried oregano
½ tsp	garlic powder or 3 cloves of crushed garlic
2 cups	torn fresh spinach
6 slices	French bread, bias-sliced ½ inch thick
6 slices	Canadian-style bacon, cut 1/8 inch thick.
6	cherry tomatoes, quartered
6 slices	Swiss cheese

- Preheat the broiler. Stir together the mayonnaise or salad dressing; thyme, basil, or oregano; and garlic powder. Toss with the spinach. Spread spinach mixture on 1 side of each bread slice.

- Place bread slices, spinach side up, on the unheated rack of the broiler pan. Place bacon slices and cherry tomatoes quarters atop spinach mixture.

- Broil bread slices about 3 inches from heat for 2 to 3 minutes or until heated through. Top the Swiss cheese slices; broil about 1 minute more until cheese just starts to melt. Serves three.

Poached B.C Salmon with Zucchini Mayonnaise

Thanks to Bill B. of Vancouver, B.C.

4 pieces	Fresh B.C. salmon, cod, halibut, or shark steaks cut to 1 to 1 ¼ inches thick.
½ cup	dry white wine
½ tsp	dried white wine
½ small	zucchini, finely chopped (about ½ cup)
¼ cup	mayonnaise *or* salad dressing
¼ cup	plain yogurt
2 tbsp	frozen snipped chives
	Fresh Radishes (optional)
	Steamed pea pods (optional)

- In a large skillet combine wine, tarragon, and 1½ cups water. Bring just to boiling. Carefully add fish. Return to boiling; reduce heat. Cover and simmer just till fish flakes with a fork (allow 8 to 12 minutes for 1-inch-thick fish steaks and 10 to 15 minutes for 1-¼ inch-fish steaks). Remove the fish steaks from wine mixture and drain thoroughly on paper towels.

- Meanwhile for sauce, in a small bowl stir together the zucchini, mayonnaise or salad dressing, yogurt, and snipped chives.

- To serve, arrange fish steaks on 4 dinner plates. Spoon some of the sauce over each fish steak. Serve with fresh radishes and steamed pea pods. Makes 4 servings.

Indian Delight

Poori - Deep Fried Puffy Bread

Sent to us from Sherry G. & family, Tacoma, Washington

- Stir 8-oz whole wheat flour, salt and 1 tbsp oil together and add enough water to make fairly stiff dough. Cover with plastic wrap and chill for 30 minutes.

- Divide the dough into small (walnut-size) balls. Flatten each one with the palm of your hand, then roll into a 4-inch circle.

- Heat oil over a moderate heat. Deep-fry the Poori on both sides until they puff up. Remove from the pan and drain off excess oil on paper towel. Serve hot, as an accompaniment with your favorite curry dish.

Asian Flair: East-West Fusion

These dishes are delicious and extremely easy to prepare. Some of the hottest restaurants in North America are serving this growing trend mix of American/Asian cuisine, and it will delight any apprehensive International Guest.

Kung Pao Chicken

Our family favorite   Go ahead, try it!

5 tbsp	soy sauce
2-½ tsp	minced fresh ginger
5 tsp	sherry (optional)
3 ½ tsp	cornstarch
2-5	minced fresh garlic cloves
2 tbsp	rice wine vinegar
¼ tsp	salt
3-5 lb	chicken wings (cut into 1-½ inch pieces)
4 tbsp	chicken broth
1 ½ tbsp	brown sugar
4 tbsp	vegetable oil
1-2 tsp	chili sauce or 4-6 dried chili peppers
3	green onions
1 tsp	sesame oil
1/3 cup	salted peanuts

Kung Pao Chicken cont'd

- For marinade, combine 3 teaspoons of soy sauce, 1 tsp ginger, 2 tsp of the sherry, 2 tsp of the cornstarch; add garlic, vinegar and the salt in a large bowl. Mix well.

- Add chicken and mix well to coat pieces. Cover and let it sit in refrigerator for least 2 hours.

- Combine remaining soy sauce, sherry; cornstarch, chicken broth and sugar. Mix well and set aside.

- Heat 1 tbsp oil in wok over medium heat. Add sesame seeds and cook until golden brown (do not burn). Remove from wok and set aside.

- Heat remaining oil in wok over medium heat. Add chili sauce or peppers and stir-fry about ½ minute.

- Increase heat to high. Add chicken and marinade and stir-fry 3-4 minutes.

- Add remaining ginger and continue to stir-fry until chicken is cooked through, 1-2 minutes more.

- Add onions and sesame oil to wok. Stir in cornstarch mixture, and add to wok; cook and stir until sauce thickens.

- Sprinkle with sesame seeds. Serve hot with your favorite rice and enjoy!

Chinese Beef with Noodles

This recipe comes from the Weathering Homestay of Seattle, Washington, and is their all time favorite dish on Asian night at their house.

8 oz	Chinese-style thin egg noodles, cooked and drained
½ cup	water
3 tsp	soy sauce
¼ tsp	salt
2 tsp	instant chicken bouillon granules
1 pound	beef romp steak, trimmed
6 tbsp	vegetable oil,
6	green onions, diagonally sliced
1 piece	fresh ginger (about 1-inch square), pared and thinly sliced
2 cloves	garlic, crushed

- Place a clean towel over wire cooling racks; spread cooked noodles evenly over towel. Let dry.

- Combine water, 2 tsp of the soy sauce, salt and bouillon granules in a small bowl.

- Cut beef across the grain into thin strips about 2 inches long.

- Heat 4 tbsp of the oil in wok or large frying pan over high heat. Add noodles and stir-fry 3 minutes.

- Pour water-soy mixture over noodles; toss until noodles are completely coated, about 2 minutes. Transfer noodles to serving dish; keep warm.

- Heat remaining 2 tbsp oil in wok over high heat. Add beef, onions, ginger, garlic and remaining 1 tsp soy sauce.

- Stir-fry until beef is cooked through, about 5 minutes, spoon meat mixture over noodles.

- Serve with stir-fried vegetables. Serves 4.

Bow to Japan!

<u>Sukiyaki</u>

Yield 4 servings. Recipe may be doubled.

1½ lbs	Beef tenderloin or sirloin
1 cup	bamboo shoots
2 medium	onions, coarsely chopped
1 cup	fresh mushrooms, sliced
6	Green onion tops, cut in 1-inch pieces
2 cups	Chinese cabbage, cut in ½-inch by 2-inch strips
½ cup	sugar
½ cup	apple juice or sauterne wine
½ cup	water
½ cup	soy sauce
2 tbsp	vegetable oil
½ cup	salted cashews

- Slice meat into paper-thin strips (across the grain). Chop vegetables.

- Arrange meat and chopped vegetables on large platter or tray, keeping each item separate.

- Pre-measure sugar, apple juice, water and soy sauce into separate small dishes and keep handy.

- Preheat large skillet. Add beef and sauté until brown.

- Stir in vegetables (except green onion tops) and cook for 10 minutes, tossing gently to prevent sticking.

- Add apple juice mixture, green onion tops and cashews, and stir.

- Serve immediately on a bed of rice.

Sushi (Rice Sandwich)

This is a very simple version of sushi taught to me by my Homestay student Yulie of Japan. Try it with your favorite fish or vegetables for fillings!

3 cups	Japanese style sticky rice
¼ cup	sweet rice vinegar
½ tsp	Salt/pepper (optional)

Fillings:

1 can	crab meat mixed with 1 tsp of Japanese mayo; or
1 package	imitation crab cake (cut in to ¼-inch thick long thin strips)
1 stick	celery (very thinly sliced in long strips)
4	green onions (very thinly sliced in long strips)
¼	avocado (optional -- cut into fine thin strips)
4 tbsp	Japanese mayo
2 tsp	prepared wasabi
8 sheets	seaweed
1	sushi mat

Sushi (Rice Sandwich) cont'd

- Cook rice in 6 cups of water, according to package directions. Transfer the rice to a large mixing bowl; add vinegar and salt mix thoroughly with a wooden spoon. Set aside to cool.

- Prepare fillings, slicing everything into thin, long strips.

- Place a sheet of seaweed on a bamboo sushi mat. Spread 1/8 of prepared rice over half of the seaweed sheet.

- Spread a thin layer of Japanese mayo over top of rice as if you were buttering a piece of bread.

- Spread a very thin layer of wasabi over mayo. Be careful not to use too much, as this is a hot touch for your taste buds!

- Place the crabmeat or fishcake in strips on top of the rice, and then put side by side a row of celery, green onions and avocado.

- Start rolling the seaweed sheet over within the mat to produce a roll. Squeeze gently to compress the rice – but not too much to squish it.

- Carefully remove the mat. The sushi should looks like a long tube. Cut the rice roll into 1-inch (1.5 cm) pieces.

- Serve with your favorite hot green tea.

That's Italian!

Chow Down Italian

This went over big at my house and easy to serve to all International Guests, never was there a drop left!

<u>Basic Tomato Sauce</u>

3 tbsp	Olive oil
salt/pepper	to taste
2 medium	onions, chopped
1-28 oz can	whole tomatoes in juice
3-4 cloves	garlic minced
2-28 oz can	crushed tomatoes
1 to 1-½ lbs	ground beef
½ cup	fresh basil
Dash or two	your favorite hot sauce
2-3	Italian sausages - sweet or hot (the hotter the better)

- Heat olive oil in large, heavy saucepan over low heat, and slowly sauté the onions, stirring often. Cook until translucent - Do not burn.

- Add garlic, and cook until soft, about 4 minutes. Do not allow the garlic to brown.

- Add ground beef, sausage, and salt /pepper to taste to sauce pan.

- Increase the heat, brown the meat until it is no longer pink. When the meat is cooked, pour off about ¾ of the fat.

- Add the whole and crushed tomatoes, salt and pepper to taste, basil and a dash or two of your favorite hot sauce.

- Reduce heat and simmer 1 to 2 hours (the longer the better). Stir often!

- Serve with your favorite pasta and fresh bread!

The fresher the ingredients ... the better the flavor!
Choose fresh tomatoes and garlic for a mouthwatering result!

Crepes of Italy

1 cup	all-purpose flour
4	eggs
1 tbsp	olive oil
1 tsp	salt
1 cup	water

Ricotta Filling

1 lb	ricotta cheese
2	eggs
½ cup	chopped flat leaf parsley
1 cup	Parmesan cheese
	Salt and pepper to taste
4 cups	shredded mozzarella cheese
4 to 6 cups	tomato sauce

- Make the crepes by combining the flour, eggs, olive oil, salt and water in a medium bowl. Stir until smooth.

- Heat a small skillet over medium-high heat and lightly brush it with olive oil.

- Ladle just enough batter into the pan to thinly cover the bottom.

- Cook until the top is set and the bottom is slightly golden, about 30 seconds.

- Transfer the crepes to wax or parchment paper. You may stack them with layers of paper between them.

- Repeat the cooking process until all of the batter is used, stirring well before pouring each crepe.

- Allow cooling.

- Fill and roll each crepe with Ricotta filling.

- Place the rolled crepes in a slightly oiled baking pan.

- Pour your favorite tomato sauce over the crepes.

- Bake for 20 minutes in a preheated oven at 350° Fahrenheit.

- Serve with your favorite salad and fresh bread.

Vegetarian Lasagna

Thanks from Judith & Lorne B. of California

1 package	lasagna noodles
½ cup	chopped onion
1 tbsp	olive oil
1 cup	grated carrot
2 cups	sliced mushrooms
1-28 oz. can	tomato sauce
1-6 oz. can	tomato paste
½ cup	chopped pitted olives
1½ tsp	oregano
3-5 cloves	crushed garlic
2 cups	ricotta cheese or creamed cottage cheese
1 lb	shredded Monterey Jack cheese or Mozzarella cheese
¼ cup	grated Parmesan Cheese
2 packages	frozen spinach

<u>*Vegetarian Lasagna cont'd*</u>

- Cooked lasagna noodles according to package directions.

- Sauté onion until in olive oil until translucent.

- Add carrots and mushrooms and cook until tender.

- Stir in tomato sauce, tomato paste, olives and oregano.

- Place a small amount of sauce in the bottom of a deep baking dish or lasagna pan.

- Arrange a layer of 1/3 of noodles in bottom of pan. Follow with more layers of:

- Layer 1/3 ricotta cheese or cottage cheese

- Layer 1/3 spinach

- Layer 1/3 tomato sauce

- Layer 1/3 Monterey Jack cheese

- Repeat each of the above layers two more times.

- Sprinkle the Parmesan cheese on top. Garnish with bits of spinach and olives.

- Bake at 375° Fahrenheit for 30 minutes.

- Serve with fresh bread and ENJOY!!!

Mmmm! Finishing Touches

<u>Peanut Butter Cookies</u>

With thanks from Rob and Diane B. Of Coquitlam, B.C

½ cup	butter
½ cup	brown sugar
½ cup	granulated sugar
1	egg
½ cup	peanut butter
½ tsp	salt
½ tsp	baking soda
1 cup	all-purpose flour
½ tsp	vanilla

- Cream butter; add sugars gradually, beating until creamy.

- Mix in egg, peanut butter, salt and baking soda and vanilla.

- Blend in flour, slowly, and mix well.

- Roll into small balls (or drop by tablespoons) and place on a greased cookie sheet.

- Press the balls flat with a floured fork.

- Bake in moderate oven (350° Fahrenheit) for 10-12 minutes.

- Yield: 4½– 5 dozen.

<u>Homemade Oatmeal Chocolate Chip Cookies</u>

Many thanks from long time Homestay hosts in Sydney, Judy & Jim K.

2 cups	melted butter
2 cups	white sugar
2 cups	brown sugar
4	eggs
2 tsp	vanilla
1 tsp	salt
2 tsp	baking soda
2 tsp	baking powder
4 cups	all-purpose flour
5 cups	blended oatmeal
1 cup	milk
1 package	chocolate chips

- In a large bowl mix the butter and sugars until well blended.

- Add vanilla and eggs and mix well.

- In a separate bowl, mix flour, oatmeal, salt, baking powder and baking soda.

- Blend together the dry mixture and the wet mixture.

- Add the chocolate chips and mix again.

- Drop by teaspoon onto a cookie-baking sheet.

- Bake at 375° Fahrenheit for 12-15 minutes, or until sides are golden brown.

- Jim says, "Serve warm! Yummy!"

- A great treat to surprise your Guest with in the evening.

Mexican Trifle

This was sent to us from a former Guest from Mexico.

¼ cup	sugar
1 tbsp	cornstarch
½ tsp	salt
2 cups	milk
2	eggs, slightly beaten
1 tsp	vanilla
4 cups	pound cake (see index)
4 tbsp	brandy
4 tbsp	apricot preserves
½ cup	whipped cream
1 tbsp	confectioners' sugar
	Grated semisweet chocolate
	Toasted silvered almonds
1	pound cake

Mexican Trifle cont'd

- Make the custard first. Combine sugar, cornstarch and salt in medium saucepan.

- Stir in milk until well blended.

- Cook over medium heat, stirring constantly, until custard mixture boils. At this point, it will be quite thin.

- Add a little of the sauce to the eggs (to slightly heat the eggs) and beat well.

- Add mixture to rest of sauce in pan and cook, stirring constantly, until mixture starts to bubble, then stir in vanilla.

- Remove from heat and cool, covered with waxed paper.

- Cut pound cake into 2-inch cubes. Place cake cubes in glass bowl and sprinkle with 3 tablespoon of brandy (optional) drizzled with preserves. Pour custard over cake cubes.

- Whip the cream with confectioner's sugar until stiff. Fold in 1 tbsp of brandy (optional).

- Top cake and custard with whipped cream. Garnish with grated chocolate and almonds.

- Cover and chill several hours before serving.

- Yield 4 to 6 servings.

Tempura Ice-Cream Balls

Thanks from the home of Wendy and Dennis L. of Burnaby, B.C.

2 cups	oil for frying
4	ice-cream balls frozen very; very hard (any flavor)
Tempura Batter	Purchase or make
	Sugar and cinnamon OR powdered sugar

- Heat oil to medium high.

- Remove balls from freezer; immediately dip into tempura batter.

- Fry until golden brown.

- Serve immediately, sprinkled with cinnamon and sugar or powdered sugar.

- Yield 4 servings.

My Favourite Recipe

More Information

Be sure to visit our web-site at www.homestaycentral.com for the latest tips, useful information, contacts, recipes, and much more!

You're Invited!

Do you have a question to field to other homestay Hosts or Guests? Or perhaps you have some interesting stories. We would love to hear from you!

Visit our discussion board/blog at www.homestaycentral.com/blog.

Coming Soon!

A useful guide full of tips and suggestions for the International Guest or Student staying at a Homestay!

Homestay 101 for Students

Check our website for the most up-to-date information

www.homestaycentral.com

How to Order Homestay 101 for Hosts

There are three convenient ways to order **Homestay 101 for Hosts.**

 Call or fax   604-931-2497

 Email us at   sales@homestaycentral.com

 Instant Download!   Order on-line and download to your home computer instantly. Visit our website:

www.homestaycentral.com

Special Offer for Schools & Organizations

☑ Advertise your link inside this book and on our website

☑ Custom covers with your company name

☑ Volume order discounts available!

For more information regarding school and agency advertising contact us at: sales@homestaycentral.com

---